世遗之城：泉州

QUANZHOU: A WORLD HERITAGE CIT

世遗之城——
宋元中国的世界海洋商贸中心

Quanzhou:
Emporium of the World in Song-Yuan China

中共泉州市委宣传部　编

海峡出版发行集团 | 福建人民出版社
THE STRAITS PUBLISHING & DISTRIBUTING GROUP | FUJIAN PEOPLE'S PUBLISHING HOUSE

目 录

Contents

引 言

1991 年 2 月 14 日，马年除夕，联合国教科文组织海上丝绸之路国际考察团乘坐由阿曼国王提供的“和平号”考察船，驶进泉州后渚港，给泉州辞旧迎新的传统节日增添了许多国际化色彩。来自亚洲、非洲、美洲、欧洲等地的专家学者，考察泉州古港古城、文物史迹、现代企业，走进古厝老宅，品尝地道闽南菜，沉浸式体验中国古老而现代的新春佳节。

对泉州丰富历史底蕴进行为期六天的考察和学术研讨后，考察团成员发自肺腑地向世界宣告，泉州整个城市是海上丝绸之路博物馆的完美体现，在泉州考察是整个考察活动中非常重要的阶段，丝绸之路是经济文化交流之路、和平发展友谊之路，泉州在海上丝绸之路上将发挥重要作用。

Introduction

On February 14, 1991, the eve of the Chinese New Year, the international team of the UNESCO Maritime Route Expedition arrived at Houzhu Port of Quanzhou on a cruise ship called "Fulk Al Salamah," provided by the Sultan of Oman. Their visit added an international touch to Quanzhou while people were celebrating the traditional festival of bidding farewell to the old and welcoming the new. Experts and scholars from Asia, Africa, the Americas, and Europe explored the ancient port and city of Quanzhou, its cultural relics and historical sites, modern enterprises, ancient buildings, and tasted authentic Minnan (literally meaning "southern Fujian") cuisine. They immersed themselves in the celebration of the Spring Festival with amalgam of the ancient and the modern.

After a six-day exploration and academic discussions on Quanzhou's rich historical heritage, the members of the expedition team sincerely declared to the world that the entire city of Quanzhou is a perfect representation of the Maritime Silk Roads Museum, and that the exploration of Quanzhou is a crucial phase of the entire expedition. The Silk Roads are routes of economic and cultural exchange, peaceful development and friendship. Quanzhou will play an important role on the Maritime Silk Road.

为了纪念这次盛况，考察团在著名的九日山祈风石刻——记录宋代政府为海外贸易商舶举行祈风仪式的摩崖石刻旁留下一方英文石刻，石刻上写道："……作为朝圣者，我们既重温这古老的祈祷，也带来了各国人民和平的信息，这也正是联合国教科文组织丝绸之路——对话之路综合研究项目的最终目标。为此，特留下这块象征友谊与对话的石刻。"

宋元时期，泉州有着当时世界上先进的水陆交通体系和制度保障、备受青睐的出口商品，以及和谐相处的多元社群。享誉世界的刺桐港帆樯林立，繁忙的小舢板在大船与码头之间接驳商货；佛寺、道观、民间宫庙与印度教寺、清真寺、天主教堂交错分布在城市中；大街小巷穿梭着印度人、阿拉伯人、波斯人、欧洲人等，各种语言与本地方言交汇着飘荡在城市上空……

To commemorate this grand occasion, the expedition team left an English inscription next to the renowned inscription recording ceremonies to pray for propitious winds to aid the merchant ships engaging in overseas trade, held by Song Dynasty (960—1279) government in Jiuri Mountain. It reads: "... a new inscription illustrating friendship and dialogue ... We, ... are here as pilgrims not only to renew that age-old prayer but also to carry the message of peace between peoples, which is the ultimate aim of the UNESCO Integral Study of the Silk Roads: Roads of Dialogue."

During the Song and Yuan dynasties (960—1368), Quanzhou possessed an advanced water and land transportation system, well-developed institutional guarantee as a thriving port city. It was renowned for its favored export goods and diverse and harmonious multicultural communities. The famous Zayton Port ("Zayton" is another name for ancient Quanzhou) was adorned with numerous sails, bustling small boats shuttling between large ships and the docks. Temples, mosques, and churches scattered throughout the city for the Buddhists, Taoists, people holding folk beliefs, Hindus, Muslims and Christians. Various other languages could be heard mingling with the local dialect as people from different backgrounds—Indian, Arabian, Persian, and European, etc.—filled the streets and alleys, creating a multicultural atmosphere.

1991 年 2 月 17 日至 20 日举行的“泉州‘中国与海上丝绸之路’国际学术讨论会”。（成冬冬 摄）
" INTERNATIONAL SEMINAR ON CHINA AND THE MARITIME ROUTES OF THE SILK ROADS QUANZHOU "
from February 17 to February 20 in 1991. (Photo by Cheng Dongdong)

联合国教科文组织海上丝绸之路国际考察团在九日山留下的石刻。（黄国炎 摄）
The English inscription in Jiuri Mountain by the international team of the UNESCO Maritime Route Expedition. (Photo by Huang Guoyan)

今天，收藏在泉州海外交通史博物馆的宋元时期外国侨民遗留的碑刻，写着阿拉伯文、波斯文、拉丁文、八思巴文、泰米尔文，还能见到汉语入门时写出的略显稚气的汉字和熟练掌握汉语时创作的书法作品等，印证了当时泉州的国际化程度。港口、桥梁、航标塔、陶瓷窑、冶铁炉和充满异域风情的建筑，穿越千年，与现代人的生活相依相守，让我们感受宋元时期世界海洋商贸的繁盛，以及泉州开放包容的城市精神。

2021 年 7 月 25 日，泉州再次受到世界瞩目。联合国教科文组织将“泉州：宋元中国的世界海洋商贸中心”列入《世界遗产名录》，22 处文化遗产点闪耀世界。在全球合作与竞争、开放与隔阂并存的时代，具有突出普遍价值的“海港模式”——泉州世界文化遗产，有助于我们思考海洋、商贸、多元、和谐、开放的内涵和价值。

2021 年 7 月，第 44 届世界遗产大会在福州举行。“泉州：宋元中国的世界海洋商贸中心”顺利通过审议，成功列入《世界遗产名录》。（陈英杰 摄）

"Quanzhou: Emporium of the World in Song-Yuan China" approved and inscribed on the World Heritage List in the 44th session of the World Heritage Committee held in Fuzhou in July, 2021. (Photo by Chen Yingjie)

Today, the steles bearing inscriptions left behind by foreign residents during the Song-Yuan period, preserved in the Quanzhou Maritime Museum, bear witness to how cosmopolitan the city was at that time. The inscriptions are written in Arabic, Persian, Latin, Phags-pa, and Tamil, and laboriously written Chinese characters by those who had just started to learn Chinese and skillfully executed Chinese calligraphy by those who had been good at Chinese can also be seen. Ports, bridges, lighthouses, ceramic kilns, iron smelters, and buildings in exotic styles have survived the passage of time, coexisting with the lives of modern people, allowing us to experience the grandeur of world maritime trade in the Song-Yuan period and the open and inclusive spirit of Quanzhou.

On July 25, 2021, Quanzhou once again drew global attention as UNESCO included "Quanzhou: Emporium of the World in Song-Yuan China" on the World Heritage List, shining the spotlight on its 22 cultural heritage sites. In an era of global cooperation and competition, openness and isolation, the "port model" of Quanzhou as a World Cultural Heritage site with outstanding universal value will help us contemplate the meaning and value of the ocean, trade, diversity, harmony, and openness.

位于龟山湾附近的刺桐树。（陈起拓 摄）
An Erythrina tree near Guishan Bay. (Photo by Chen Qituo)

unesco

World Heritage Convention

CONVENTION CONCERNING
THE PROTECTION OF
THE WORLD CULTURAL
AND NATURAL HERITAGE

The World Heritage Committee
has inscribed

Quanzhou: Emporium of the World
in Song-Yuan China

on the World Heritage List

Inscription on this List confirms the outstanding universal value of a cultural or natural property which requires protection for the benefit of all humanity

DATE OF INSCRIPTION

31 July 2021

Audrey Azoulay

DIRECTOR-GENERAL
OF UNESCO

泉州世界遗产证书。（中共泉州市委宣传部 供图）

Quanzhou World Heritage Certificate. (Courtesy of the Publicity Department of the CPC Quanzhou Municipal Committee)

国之东南，向海而生

A Coastal City in the Southeast of China

泉州在哪里

The Location of Quanzhou

泉州兴起的千年脉络

Quanzhou’s Millennium Development

泉州在哪里

19 世纪末，曾有西方学者提出疑问，那个非常繁华美丽的“刺桐城”究竟在中国的哪里？此问引起当时汉学家的兴趣，也带动了国际学术界持续数十年对泉州的关注和研究。随着文献资料的挖掘和泉州城内一件件文物的出土，尤其是宋元石刻上清晰的“刺桐”阿拉伯碑文，人们确定世界东端那个极度昌盛的刺桐城就是现在的泉州。

刺桐，泉州别称。五代时期，为适应海外贸易需要，泉州扩城建设，在“州之城墙，傍植刺桐环绕”。刺桐树开花时满枝一簇簇、红灿灿的花朵，甚是美艳。来到这里的外国人将“刺桐”一词的泉州方言转译为“Zayton”，后经伟大的旅行家马可 · 波罗、伊本 · 白图泰的传播，刺桐城成为人们心目中一个充满财富和追逐梦想的地方，蜚声世界。

刺桐花是泉州市市花。（陈起拓 摄）
Quanzhou's city flower: Erythrina variegata. (Photo by Chen Qituo)

The Location of Quanzhou

At the end of the 19th century, Western scholars raised a question about the whereabouts of a prosperous and beautiful city in China called "Zayton." This question piqued the interest of Sinologists at the time and sparked decades-long attention and research on Quanzhou in the international academic community. With the exploration of historical documents and the excavation of cultural relics within the city, particularly the clear Arabic inscriptions mentioning the city on Song and Yuan stone carvings, it was determined that the flourishing city referred to as "Zayton" was none other than present-day Quanzhou.

"Zayton" is another name for Quanzhou. During the Five Dynasties period (907—960), Quanzhou was expanded to accommodate overseas trade. "Erythrina variegata (known as 'Citong' in Chinese pinyin) were planted around the city walls." When the Erythrina trees bloomed, their branches were filled with clusters of bright red flowers, presenting a beautiful sight. Visitors from overseas translated "Citong" in Quanzhou dialect into "Zayton." Through the dissemination by renowned travelers such as Marco Polo and Ibn Battuta, "Zayton" became synonymous with wealth and dreams, gaining worldwide fame.

泉州位于中国东南海滨。古代泉州城里沟渠纵横、池塘密布、水系环绕，仿若在海中。泉州的很多地名里有“浦”“津”“淮”等字眼，就是因为城市沿江靠海、水域发达。大概由于水资源十分充沛，人们相信泉州的名称是源于泉州的母亲山——清源山上长流不断的虎乳泉。其实，泉州之名在唐景云二年（711）才开始被今天的泉州使用，颇为有趣的是，在这之前，“泉州”指的是现在的福州。

泉州市现辖鲤城、丰泽、洛江、泉港 4 个区，晋江、石狮、南安 3 个县级市，惠安、安溪、永春、德化、金门（待统一）5 个县和泉州经济技术开发区、泉州台商投资区。全市土地面积 11,015 平方千米（含金门县），2024 年末常住人口 891.4 万人（不含金门县）。

清源山上的虎乳泉。（陈英杰 摄）
Huru Spring on Mount Qingyuan. (Photo by Chen Yingjie)

Quanzhou is located on the southeastern coast of China. The ancient city of Quanzhou was crisscrossed with canals, dotted with ponds, and surrounded by waterways, giving it the appearance of being immersed in the sea. Many place names in Quanzhou contain words such as "pu," "jin," and "huai," indicating its proximity to rivers and seas and its developed waterways. Perhaps due to the abundant water resources, people believed that the name "Quanzhou" originated from the continuously flowing Huru Spring on Mount Qingyuan, the mother mountain of Quanzhou. In fact, the name "Quanzhou" began to be used for the present-day Quanzhou in 711. Interestingly, before that, "Quanzhou" referred to what is now Fuzhou.

Quanzhou City currently administers four districts: Licheng, Fengze, Luojiang, and Quangang, as well as three county-level cities: Jinjiang, Shishi, and Nan'an, and it also includes five counties: Hui'an, Anxi, Yongchun, Dehua, and Jinmen (to be reunified), as well as the Quanzhou Economic and Technological Development Zone and the Quanzhou Taiwan Business Investment Zone. Its land area covers 11,015 square kilometers (Jinmen included). The city has a permanent population of 8.914 million at the end of 2024 (Jinmen not included).

泉州依山面海，西北高东南低，有山地、丘陵、台地和沿海平原等地貌。西北部的戴云山海拔 1,856 米，是泉州境内最高山峰。再往西北深入闽中腹地，山外有山，一层一叠的丘陵山地绵延至闽赣交界的武夷山脉，所以古代泉州的内陆交通极为不便。然而，层层叠叠的山脉却能挡住从西伯利亚南下的寒流。泉州属亚热带海洋性季风气候，这里常年降水丰沛，温暖湿润，冬季比同纬度其他地区气温略高，又因为晋江喇叭状入海口吸引海洋水汽深入内地，夏季又比同纬度其他地区气温略低。温润的气候使泉州又拥有“温陵”的别称。

晋江和洛阳江遥遥相望，自西北向东南奔流入海。它们不是大江大河，却是哺育泉州的母亲河，它们环抱着开阔的泉州平原，养育了一代又一代的泉州人民，孕育了泉州灿烂的世界文化遗产。

泉州枕山面海，气候温暖湿润，别称“温陵”。（陈英杰 摄）
Quanzhou, nestling against the mountains and facing the sea, enjoys a warm and humid climate, also known as "Warm Hills." (Photo by Chen Yingjie)

Quanzhou is located with mountains to the northwest and the sea to the southeast, featuring a varied topography of mountains, hills, tablelands, and coastal plains. The highest peak within Quanzhou's borders is Mount Daiyun with an elevation of 1,856 meters. As one moves further into the inland regions toward the northwest, there are layer upon layer of hills and mountains extending to Mount Wuyi on the border between Fujian Province and Jiangxi Province, making ancient Quanzhou's inland transportation quite inconvenient. However, these layered mountains serve as a barrier against the cold air masses coming from Siberia. Quanzhou has a subtropical maritime monsoon climate, characterized by high humidity and abundant rainfall. The winter temperatures in Quanzhou are slightly higher compared to other areas at the same latitude. Additionally, the trumpet-shaped Jinjiang River estuary attracts marine moisture inland, resulting in slightly lower temperatures in Quanzhou during the summer compared to other areas at the same latitude. The mild climate has earned Quanzhou the nickname "Wenling" (literally meaning "warm hills").

The Jinjiang River and the Luoyang River, accompanying each other from afar, flow from the northwest to the southeast, eventually reaching the sea. Although they are not large, they are the mother rivers of Quanzhou. These rivers embrace the relatively spacious Quanzhou Plain, nurturing generations of Quanzhou people and fostering Quanzhou's splendid world cultural heritage.

泉州陆地在伸向海洋时，形成了曲折的海岸线和平静的海湾。海湾是舟船避风避浪的安身之处，泉州绵长海岸线上的各个海湾经历代开发，逐渐出现了大大小小的港口。最著名的“三湾十二港”，在宋元时期各领风骚、共同发展，形成繁华的港口群，“刺桐港”的盛名享誉世界。

泉州，由此出发。

The land of Quanzhou extends toward the ocean, forming a winding coastline and tranquil bays. These bays provide shelter for boats and ships, and over the generations, the development of the bays along Quanzhou's extensive coastline has led to the emergence of numerous ports. The most famous among them are the "Three Bays and Twelve Ports." During the Song and Yuan dynasties, these ports each flourished and developed together, forming a prosperous port cluster known as the "Zayton Port," renowned worldwide.

Thus, from Quanzhou, the journey begins.

泉州漫长的海岸线。（陈英杰 摄）
Quanzhou's long coastline. (Photo by Chen Yingjie)

泉州兴起的千年脉络

早期开发。泉州先民很早就在此耕耘和生活，已经发现的几十处新石器时代文化遗存，比较清晰地反映了泉州先民的生活印记。在永春、安溪等地，出土了许多石锛、石斧等磨制农耕工具，石矛、石镞等制作精良的武器，以及陶杯、陶豆、陶罐等生活用具；在南安、永春等地的新石器时代遗址中，有稻草、稻秆、谷粒的痕迹；在晋江沿岸和滨海地区有多处贝丘遗址，堆积了大量人类食余弃置的贝壳。

这些分布甚广、数量可观的新石器时代生产工具、生活用具和作物，展现了三四千年前泉州先民的生活场景，农耕和渔猎是他们主要的生产活动，稻米是他们辛勤劳作的回报，贝类、鱼类是大自然馈赠他们的美味。

福建的青铜时代似乎比其他地方来得晚一些。1974 年 5 月，在南安大盈寨山发现西周时期的青铜器，是福建省青铜器出土数量较为集中的一次，包括农耕和砍伐工具——铜锛，青铜制的戈、矛、戚、匕首等武器，八个渐次大小的铜铃，上面分别装饰着弦纹、几何纹、云雷纹、波浪纹等，同时发现了一件磨制美观的淡青色玉戈和四件制作精良的淡青色玉璜。铜铃、玉戈和玉璜除了具有鲜明的地方特征外，其样式和纹饰与中原地区很相似。南安大盈寨山遗址带给我们两个重要的信息：一是这批文物可能来自墓葬，从已发现礼器的规格判断，墓主应当是军队中的武官或者奴隶主；二是相比中原地区，福建进入青铜时代的时间较晚、制造技艺的发展滞后，但泉州在西周时期就开始与中原地区接触和交流。

新石器时代的石锛、石斧等。（段燕飞 摄）
Stone adzes, axes, and other tools from the Neolithic period. (Photo by Duan Yanfei)

Quanzhou's Millennium Development

Early Development. The ancestors of Quanzhou cultivated and lived in this area from very early times. The dozens of Neolithic cultural sites that have been discovered clearly reflect the life of Quanzhou's early inhabitants. Numerous ground agricultural implements such as stone adzes and stone axes, finely crafted weapons like stone spears and arrowheads, along with pottery vessels like cups, pedestal dishes, and jars, have been unearthed in places like Yongchun and Anxi. Traces of straw, rice stalks, and grain have been found in Neolithic sites in Nan'an, Yongchun and other places, while numerous shell mounds, containing a large number of discarded shells from human consumption, are scattered along the banks of Jinjiang River and in coastal areas.

These widely distributed and abundant Neolithic production tools, daily utensils, and crops showcase the living scenes of Quanzhou's ancient inhabitants from three to four thousand years ago. Farming and fishing were their main production activities, with rice being the rewarding result of their hard work, and shellfish and fish, the bountiful gifts from nature.

The Bronze Age seems to have arrived relatively late in Fujian, China. In May 1974, in Dayingzhai Hill in Nan'an, bronze artifacts from the Western Zhou period (1046 B.C.—771 B.C.) were discovered. This excavation represents a concentrated finding of bronze artifacts in the province. The discoveries included agricultural and cutting tools such as bronze adzes, as well as bronze weapons like dagger-axes, spears, axes, and daggers. Eight bronze bells in increasing sizes were also found, adorned with various patterns of strings, geometric shapes, clouds as well as thunder, and waves. Besides, a finely polished light blue jade dagger-axe and four intricately crafted light blue *yu huang* (a semi-annular jade pendant) were also discovered. In addition to the distinct local characteristics, the styles and patterns of the bronze bells, jade dagger-axe, and jade *yu huang* were quite similar to those in the Central Plains. The Dayingzhai Hill site in Nan'an provides important information. First, these artifacts are likely from graves, and based on the identified ceremonial object specifications, the tomb occupant is believed to be a military officer or a slave owner. Second, despite Fujian's entry into the Bronze Age later than the Central Plains and thus a delayed development in manufacturing techniques, Quanzhou had, as it was, already begun its contact and exchange with the Central Plains during the Western Zhou period.

泉州青铜器制造技艺虽逊于中原，但制瓷业却相当发达，在青铜时代处于全国领先地位。“2016 年度全国十大考古新发现”之一的永春苦寨坑原始青瓷窑址，为我们揭开了这段历史。2015 年，考古人员在永春县介福乡的苦寨坑进行考古发掘，9 条依山而建的龙窑遗迹跃然出现，大量制作工艺高超、器形纹饰丰富的原始青瓷惊世瞩目。经考证，其年代大约为公元前 18 世纪中期至公元前 14 世纪末期，相当于夏朝中期至商朝中期，是我国目前已知烧造最早原始青瓷的窑址。苦寨坑原始青瓷犹如泉州陶瓷业的希望之火，点燃了泉州大地无数窑炉，生生不息，绵延至今，其中，外销陶瓷风靡于古代海上丝绸之路的磁灶窑址和德化窑址，至今得到完好保护，是世界文化遗产的组成部分。

永春苦寨坑原始青瓷窑址。（张红兴 供图）
The Kuzhaikeng Proto-Celadon Production Site in Yongchun. (Courtesy of Zhang Hongxing)

Although the bronze craftsmanship in Quanzhou may have been less advanced than that in the Central Plains, its porcelain industry was quite developed, attaining a leading position nationwide during the Bronze Age. The Kuzhaikeng Proto-Celadon Production Site in Yongchun, listed as one of the "National Top Ten Archaeological Discoveries of 2016," has revealed this historical significance. In 2015, archaeologists conducted excavations on Mount Kuzhaikeng in Jiefu Township, Yongchun County. Nine loong-shaped kiln sites built along the mountain emerged, showcasing a large number of proto-celadon ceramics with sophisticated craftsmanship and rich decorative patterns, attracting worldwide attention. Evidence shows that these ceramics were produced approximately between the mid-Xia Dynasty and mid-Shang Dynasty, from around the mid-18th century B.C. to the late 14th century B.C. This makes the Kuzhaikeng Proto-Celadon Production Site the earliest known proto-celadon kiln site in China. The proto-celadon from Kuzhaikeng was like the beacon of hope for Quanzhou's ceramic industry. It ignited numerous kilns across Quanzhou which thrived and continued to this day. Among them, the Sites of Cizao Kilns and Sites of Dehua Kilns, famous for their exported ceramics along the ancient Maritime Silk Road, are well-preserved and constitute part of the World Cultural Heritage.

泉州先民在战国晚期开始了族群的融合发展。福建古称“闽”，土著闽人是百越民族的一支。生活在江浙一带的另一支土著越人，为了躲避兵祸，一部分人来到闽地，他们强大的军事力量和先进的生产方式，深刻地影响了闽人的社会生活。卧薪尝胆而成为春秋最后一霸的越王勾践，应该没有预料到他的后代将对闽地产生不小的影响，他们与土著闽人逐渐融合，形成闽越族，并在战国晚期建立了闽越国。秦统一六国之后，闽越王无诸被削去王号，封为闽中郡君长。秦朝泉州为闽中郡所辖，汉朝属会稽郡，纳入中央王朝直接统治。

In the late Warring States period (475 B.C.—221 B.C.), the ancient inhabitants of Quanzhou began the process of integrated development of ethnic groups. The ancient name for Fujian Province was "Min," and the indigenous Min people were a branch of the *Baiyue* (various peoples who inhabited southern China in ancient times). Another indigenous group called the Yue people, who lived in the Jiangsu and Zhejiang regions, migrated to the Min area to escape warfare. Their great military strength and advanced production methods profoundly influenced the social life of the Min people. King Goujian of Yue, the last powerful marquess of the Spring and Autumn period (770 B.C.—476 B.C.) who had forced himself to sleep on sticks and taste bile to remember his hardship and finally won the victory, probably did not anticipate the significant impact his descendants would have on the Min region. Through interactions with the Min people, they gradually blended in with the local community, hence the formation of Minyue People. The Minyue Kingdom was established in the late Warring States period. After the Qin State unified the other six states, the title of the Minyue King was abolished, and Wuzhu was appointed as the Lord of Minzhong Commandery. During the Qin Dynasty (221 B.C.—206 B.C.), Quanzhou was under the jurisdiction of Minzhong Commandery, and during the Han Dynasty (206 B.C.—220 A.D.), it was part of Kuaiji Commandery, under the direct rule of the Central Court.

闽越人进一步开发泉州，他们尤善于舟、习于水，《汉书》记载：“越，方外之地，剪发文身之民也。”“处溪谷之间，篁竹之中，习于水斗，便于用舟。”《越绝书》记载闽越人“水行而山处，以船为车，以楫为马。往若飘风，去则难从”。古书将闽越人的水上生活习性描绘得十分生动形象，泉州沿江靠海的人们把这种水上生活方式一直延续了下来，其中包括史书提到的“泉郎”。北宋《太平寰宇记》中提到的“泉郎”亦称“白水郎”“游艇子”，是东晋后期卢循率领农民起义军失败后流亡的余部，他们落户泉州后有的隐于山区，有的居于海边、船上，可随时驾舟活动。“泉郎”使用的船型头尾尖翘、中间平阔，有较强的抗风浪性能，名曰“了鸟船”，已具有福船的雏形。

The people of Minyue continued to develop Quanzhou. They were adept at boating and accustomed to water. The *Book of Han* records, "In Yue, an area beyond the Central Plains, live people who have their hair cut and put tattoos on their skin." "They dwell between streams and valleys, amidst bamboo groves, and are skilled in using boats for water battles." The *Book of Yue Jue* describes the people of Minyue as "traveling on water and dwelling in mountains, using boats as vehicles and oars as horses. They come and go like a wind, which is hard for others to follow." Ancient books vividly depict the water-connected lifestyle of the Minyue people, which later continued among the people living along the rivers and near the sea in Quanzhou, including the *quan lang* mentioned in historical records. Northern Song Dynasty's *Universal Geography of the Taiping Xingguo Era* has mentioned *quan lang*, also known as *bai shui lang* or *you ting zi*. They were the surviving group of the peasant uprising army led by Lu Xun in the late Eastern Jin Dynasty (317—420) when they failed and went adrift. After settling down in Quanzhou, some of them secluded themselves in the mountains, while others lived by the seaside or on boats so that they were able to relocate by boat at any time. The boats used by the *quan lang* had pointed ends and a wide middle, providing good resistance against wind and waves. They were called *liao niao chuan* (literally meaning "bird-shaped junks") and represented the prototype of the *Fu-Chuan* (literally meaning "Fortune Vessel").

闽南首县——丰州。三国时期，孙吴政权延伸至闽地，于吴永安三年（260）设置东安县，县治在今南安丰州，归建安郡管辖。东安县是闽南地区最早设立的县一级政府机构，此时泉州已经是闽南政治、经济与文化的中心，管辖今泉州市部分地区、厦门市、莆田市以及漳州市部分地区。晋太康三年（282），东安县改名为晋安县。南朝梁天监年间，晋安县由县升级为南安郡，治所依然在丰州，管理着晋安、兰水、龙溪三县。丰州作为行政机构所在地的重要地位一直持续了 440 年，至武周久视元年（700）行政中心才迁到今鲤城区。

丰州面向晋江，背靠清源山脉，人们很早就在此聚居，泉州最古老的佛教寺庙——延福寺就建在丰州九日山下。在丰州的狮子山麓，发掘了六朝古墓葬群，墓葬出土大量青瓷、陶器，少量铁器、铜钱、铜镜、铜印等，还有弥足珍贵的纪年墓砖，“太康五年”“咸康元年”“宁康三年”“太元三年”等字清晰可辨，显示了汉人南迁、汉文化传播的历史事实。

南安丰州六朝古墓。（成冬冬 摄）
The ancient tombs of the Six Dynasties located in Fengzhou, Nan'an. (Photo by Cheng Dongdong)

Fengzhou: The First County in the South of Min (also known as southern Fujian). During the Three Kingdoms period (220—280), the Kingdom of Wu continuously extended its influence into the Min region. In 260, Dong'an County was established, with its seat in present-day Fengzhou, Nan'an, under the jurisdiction of Jian'an Commandery. Dong'an County was the earliest county-level governmental institution established in the South of Min. By this time, Quanzhou had already become the political, economic, and cultural center of southern Fujian, governing parts of present-day Quanzhou, Xiamen, Putian, and parts of Zhangzhou. In 282, Dong'an County was renamed Jin'an County. During the Tianjian era (502—519) in the Southern Liang Dynasty, Jin'an County was upgraded to Nan'an Commandery, with Fengzhou still as its governing center, administering the three counties of Jin'an, Lanshui, and Longxi. Fengzhou's status as the administrative center lasted for 440 years until the center was moved to the present-day Licheng District in 700.

Fengzhou, facing the Jinjiang River and backed by Mount Qingyuan, was the earliest settlement town in the area. The oldest Buddhist temple in Quanzhou, Yanfu Temple, was built at the foot of Jiuri Mountain in Fengzhou. A concentration of ancient tombs, dating back to the Six Dynasties period (222—589), was discovered at the foothills of Lion Hill in Fengzhou. Unearthed from these tombs were many celadon and pottery artifacts, as well as a small number of iron objects, copper coins, bronze mirrors, and bronze seals. Additionally, there are valuable tomb bricks with inscriptions indicating the years of burial, such as "the fifth year of Taikang (284)," "the first year of Xiankang (335)," "the third year of Ningkang (375)," and "the third year of Taiyuan (378)." These findings demonstrate the historical fact of the migration of Han people southward and the spread of Han culture.

“竹林七贤”之一阮咸对音乐有“神解”的才能，他精通音律，善弹一种形似古琴而颈较长的琵琶，经常与朋友弹琴饮乐。这种琵琶凭借阮咸的名声风行全国，被后人称为“阮”或“阮咸”。丰州六朝古墓出土的墓砖上还有阮咸图案，从中可以了解这一古乐器在那个时代的演变过程。

泉州第一个有历史记载的对外交通的港口——梁安港，也在丰州。南朝皇帝信奉佛教，中国与印度等佛教国度的海上交通往来渐渐兴起。印度高僧拘那罗陀受梁武帝邀请来中国传播佛法，于陈天嘉二年（561）到达泉州，从梁安港上岸。他在泉州期间，一边等候季风返回家乡，一边在九日山下的延福寺翻译《金刚经》。次年，拘那罗陀从梁安港启航南行，中途遇上台风，船漂到广州。他是目前有记载的最早来到泉州的外国人，这从一个侧面印证了泉州当时港口建设、船舶制造、海外交通的发展。

南朝阮咸纹墓砖。（成冬冬 摄）
The tomb brick with *ruan xian* pattern in the Southern Dynasties. (Photo by Cheng Dongdong)

Ruan Xian, one of the Seven Sages of the Bamboo Grove, possessed a remarkable talent for music. He was highly skilled in musical theory and excelled at playing a type of *pi pa*, a stringed instrument resembling *gu qin* (an ancient Chinese zither) but with a longer neck. Ruan Xian and his friends frequently gathered together to play music, drink and enjoy themselves. This particular *pi pa* became widely known throughout the country by virtue of Ruan Xian's reputation, and later generations even referred to it as the *ruan* or *ruan xian*. There are *ruan xian* patterns on the tomb bricks of the Six Dynasties period unearthed from the ancient tombs in Fengzhou, which demonstrate some of the evolutionary processes of the musical instrument during that era.

Fengzhou was also home to Quanzhou's first historically recorded port for overseas transportation called Liang'an Port. During the Southern Dynasties (420—589), emperors embraced Buddhism, and communications with Buddhist countries like India began to flourish. Gunarata, an eminent Indian monk, was invited to China by Emperor Wu of Liang to spread Buddhism. In 561, Gunarata arrived in Quanzhou and disembarked at Liang'an Port. While waiting for the monsoon winds to return to his homeland, he resided in Yanfu Temple at the foot of Jiuri Mountain, where he translated the *Diamond Sutra*. The following year, Gunarata set sail southward from Liang'an Port but in a typhoon he drifted to Guangzhou. He is currently the earliest recorded foreigner to have arrived in Quanzhou, which indirectly confirms the development of port construction, shipbuilding, and overseas transportation in Quanzhou during that time.

汉人南迁。中原汉人南迁持续不断，深刻影响了泉州的人口构成，加速了泉州的开发与发展。晋元康元年（291）爆发“八王之乱”，晋永嘉五年（311）爆发“永嘉之乱”，北方大地战火纷飞、生灵涂炭，许多北方人被迫逃离家乡，一部分人南迁进入泉州。《福建通志》记载：“晋永嘉二年，中州板荡，衣冠始入闽者八族，林、陈、黄、郑、詹、邱、何、胡是也。”《太平寰宇记》记载：“东晋南渡，衣冠士族多萃其地，以求安堵。”衣冠士族，原指风度翩翩、峨冠博带的官宦士绅。历史上曾有大规模的“衣冠南渡”，显然，在南迁的北方人中，不只是农民、士兵，还有大量的士族、军官等，他们长途跋涉、颠沛流离，为这片土地带来了新的文化、礼仪和技艺。

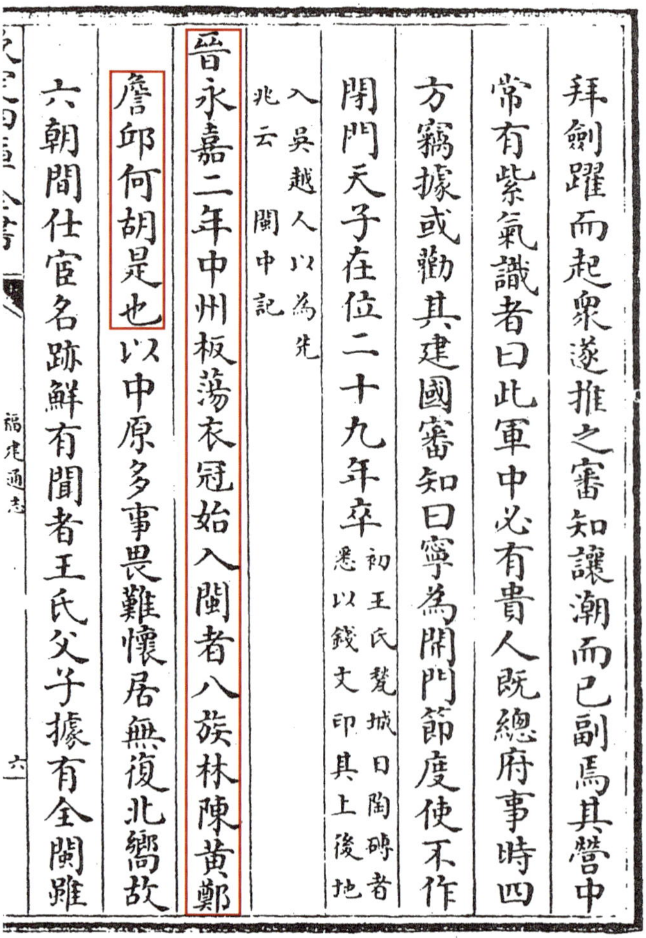
拜劍躍而起衆遂推之審知讓潮而已副焉其營中
常有紫氣識者曰此軍中必有貴人既總府事時四
方竊據或勸其建國審知曰寧為開門節度使不作
閉門天子在位二十九年卒初王氏甃城日陶磚者悉以錢文印其上後地
入吳越人以為先兆云閩中記
晉永嘉二年中州板蕩衣冠始入閩者八族林陳黃鄭
詹邱何胡是也以中原多事畏難懷居無復北嚮故
六朝間仕宦名跡鮮有聞者王氏父子據有全閩雖
福建通志　六

《福建通志》中关于八姓入闽的记载。（林瀚　供图）
A record of the eight surnames entering Min (Fujian) in *A General Gazetteer of Fujian*. (Courtesy of Lin Han)

The Han People's Southward Migration. The continuous migration of Han people from the Central Plains to the south had profoundly influenced the demographic composition of Quanzhou and accelerated its development and growth. The "Eight Princes' Rebellion" that erupted in 291, and the "Yongjia Rebellion" that broke out in 311, plunged the northern regions into turmoil and devastation, forcing many people to flee their homes. As a result, a portion of the northern population migrated southward and settled in Quanzhou. According to *A General Gazetteer of Fujian*, in 308, when chaos prevailed in the Central Plains, members of the literati and official class began to enter Fujian. They were people surnamed Lin, Chen, Huang, Zheng, Zhan, Qiu, He, and Hu. The book, *Universal Geography of the Taiping Xingguo Era*, also records that during the Eastern Jin Dynasty's migration southward, many literati and members of the noble class settled in Quanzhou in search of stability and security. The term *Yiguan Shizu* (dress code of headwear and waist belts to indicate the status as officials from the eminent family) originally referred to elegantly attired distinguished officials and gentry. Obviously, among the northerners who relocated southward, there were not only farmers and soldiers but also the literati, military officers, and other elites. After a long journey of upheaval and displacement, they finally settled in Quanzhou, enriching the local culture with their customs, social norms, and skills.

南朝梁将领侯景发动“侯景之乱”后，对江南经济和士族阶层造成了毁灭性的打击，很多江南普通百姓向南迁移至闽地避难。南安丰州发现的几十座六朝墓葬，也反映了中原和江南移民南来后聚族而居、集中族葬的生活习俗。中原汉人不仅带来了先进的犁耕、牛耕等农耕方式，纺织技术和陶瓷技艺，还带来了汉文化的审美情趣和人文修养。在南朝时期的墓砖上，佛像和僧人等人物形象惟妙惟肖，朱雀、鱼、龙、花草等图案栩栩如生。墓里还出土了壶嘴形状如鸡头的青釉鸡首壶等。

During the Southern Liang Dynasty, General Hou Jing started the "Hou Jing Rebellion," which dealt a devastating blow to the economy and the aristocratic class in Jiangnan (regions south of the Yangtze River). As a result, many common people from Jiangnan migrated southward to seek refuge in Fujian. The discovery of dozens of Six Dynasties' tombs in Fengzhou, Nan'an, also reflects the customs of people from the Central Plains and Jiangnan: clustering and burying family members as a group. The Han people from the Central Plains brought not only advanced agricultural techniques, such as plowing and ox cultivation, textile technology, and ceramic craftsmanship, but also the aesthetic tastes and humanistic cultivation of Han culture. On the tomb bricks from the Southern Dynasties, Buddhist statues as well as monks and other human figures are vividly portrayed, as well as the patterns of rosefinches, fish, loong, flowers, and grass. Various artifacts have been unearthed from these tombs, including a celadon ewer with spout shaped like a chicken head.

东晋青釉鸡首壶。（成冬冬 摄）

A celadon ewer with spout shaped like a chicken head in the Eastern Jin Dynasty. (Photo by Cheng Dongdong)

南朝青釉烛台等。（段燕飞 摄）

A celadon candle holder and other items in the Southern Dynasties. (Photo by Duan Yanfei)

日渐兴盛。中原人持续南来，推动了泉州经济进步和汉越族群融合。其间，距离丰州十多里的晋江下游冲积平原上，逐渐出现新的民居和商业聚集区，这个区域内建有福建省最早的道观元妙观和大型佛教寺庙莲花寺（也就是后来的开元寺）。武周久视元年（700），泉州州治也东迁到这个欣欣向荣的新区（现鲤城区），行政中心更靠近海港。唐景云二年（711），原“武荣州”更名为“泉州”，沿用至今。由于五代时期刺桐树在泉州广为种植，“刺桐”一度成为泉州的代名词。晚唐诗人曹松在赠别友人回泉州的诗中写道：“帝京须早入，莫被刺桐迷。”唐朝诗人陈陶也赋诗盛赞泉州：“海曲春深满郡霞，越人多种刺桐花。”作为唐代四大港口之一的泉州，着实配得上这样的夸赞。唐元和六年（811），泉州由中州升为上州，甚至被称为“富州”。

晋江是泉州人的母亲河。（陈英杰 摄）
Quanzhou's mother river: the Jinjiang River. (Photo by Chen Yingjie)

Thriving Development. The continuous migration of people from the Central Plains to the south had propelled the economic progress of Quanzhou and the integration of the Han and Yue ethnic groups. In the process, a new residential and commercial cluster gradually emerged on the alluvial plain downstream of the Jinjiang River, about a dozen *li* (a Chinese unit of distance. One *li* is equal to 500 meters) away from Fengzhou. Many famous temples were built in this area, such as the earliest Taoist temple in Fujian Province, Yuanmiao Temple, and a large Buddhist temple, Lianhua Temple, later renamed Kaiyuan Temple. In 700, the capital of Quanzhou was relocated to this thriving new area (now known as the Licheng District), bringing the administrative center closer to the port. In 711, the original "Wurongzhou" was renamed "Quanzhou," a name that has been used ever since. During the Five Dynasties period, Erythrina variegata were widely planted in Quanzhou, and "Zayton," derived from "Citong," briefly became synonymous with the city. In a poem bidding farewell to a friend returning to Quanzhou, the late Tang poet Cao Song wrote, "You must enter the imperial capital early and not be fascinated by Erythrina trees." The Tang (618—907) poet Chen Tao also composed an ode to the city of Quanzhou: "In the spring of the bay area, the entire prefecture is filled with rosy clouds, and the Yue people plant Erythrina trees in abundance." As one of the four major ports in the Tang Dynasty, Quanzhou indeed lived up to such praises. In 811, the city was upgraded from Zhongzhou (city of medium population density) to Shangzhou (city of high population density) and even referred to as "Fuzhou" (literally meaning "rich city").

唐末五代，被王审知招揽而流寓南安的著名学士韩偓这样描写当时的泉州："中华地向城边尽，外国云从岛上来。四序有花长见雨，一冬无雪却闻雷。"韩学士无意之中把中华心系海洋的气脉，以及泉州美丽的风景和宜人的气候表现得淋漓尽致。

唐初，河南光州固始人陈政、陈元光父子率军入闽，带动了一次北方汉人入闽的高潮，对泉州城市发展产生了深远影响。那时，泉潮间的"蛮獠啸乱"使中国东南动荡不安。朝廷命陈政率领府兵 3,600 人平定七闽百粤的寇乱，开拓东南土地。后来，陈政的兄长和母亲又带领 58 姓聚族而行前去支援，这是一支更加庞大的队伍。他们到漳州一带开拓边疆、保境安民、造福一方，也为泉州营造了良好的发展环境。一些部将、士兵选择在泉州安家终老，他们使闽南及周边土地免遭战火，这里成为名副其实的"乐土"。此次大迁移有官方的强力保障，参与人数众多，持续时间长，文化影响深远，闽南发展进入了快车道。唐开元年间，泉州人口已达三万七千多户，比唐初高了许多，在全闽户数的占比也较高。

During the late Tang Dynasty and the Five Dynasties period, Han Wo, a renowned scholar who was once recruited by Wang Shenzhi as a talent and settled in Nan'an, described Quanzhou at that time as follows: "The land of China extends to the edge of the city, and exotic clouds arrive from above the islands. Flowers bloom in all seasons, and rain is often seen, while not a single snowflake falls during winter, yet thunder can be periodically heard." Inadvertently, Han Wo vividly portrayed Chinese people's careful consideration of exploring the ocean, as well as the beautiful scenery and pleasant climate of Quanzhou.

In the early Tang Dynasty, Chen Zheng and his son Chen Yuanguang, from Gushi, Guangzhou, Henan, led an army into Fujian, sparking a wave of migration of Han people from the north to Fujian and exerting a profound influence on the rise of Quanzhou. During that time, the roaring riots around the border between Quanzhou and Chaozhou disrupted the stability of southeastern China. The imperial court appointed General Chen Zheng to lead a force of 3,600 soldiers to suppress the rebellions near the border between Fujian and Guangdong, and to open up the southeastern territories. Later, Chen Zheng's elder brother and mother led a larger group consisting of people from 58 surnames to provide support, forming an even more massive force. While in Zhangzhou, they pioneered the frontier, maintained border security, and did many things to benefit local people, creating a favorable environment for the growth of Quanzhou. Many of the generals and soldiers chose to settle in Quanzhou for the rest of their life. Their endeavor to protect the lands of southern Fujian and its surrounding areas from the ravages of war helped the city earn the reputation of "a land of joy." Thanks to the government's strong support, this large-scale migration involving many people lasted for a long time, resulting in a profound cultural impact and fast development of southern Fujian. By the Kaiyuan period (713—741) of the Tang Dynasty, the number of households in Quanzhou had exceeded 37,000, much higher than that of the early Tang Dynasty, accounting for a large portion of the total number of households in the entire Fujian.

唐末五代，又发生了一次影响泉州的人口迁移和开发。唐末，从河南光州固始走出的王潮、王审邽、王审知三兄弟随起义军南下入闽，因缘际会之下，王潮成了起义军的首领，在当地百姓的支持下攻克泉州。精心治泉五年后，他们积蓄了足够的力量，于唐景福二年（893）攻克福州，不久便统一全闽。泉州由王审邽管辖，他坚守王潮的治理方略，安定民众、扶助农桑，重视民生建设。他的儿子王延彬最享誉历史的名声是“招宝侍郎”。王延彬推动泉州向前发展，促进了海上贸易的繁荣。他主政期间，出发向海外的大商船，从来没有沉没的，足见此时已有制造大船和远洋航行的高超水平。当时的泉州，文物为十国之冠。

开闽三王祠内供奉着王潮、王审邽、王审知的雕像。（吴拏云 摄）
Inside the Temple of the Min Pioneers, statues of Wang Chao, Wang Shengui, Wang Shenzhi are enshrined to mark their exploring achievements. (Photo by Wu Nayun)

During the late Tang Dynasty and the Five Dynasties period, another significant migration and development occurred that influenced Quanzhou. Toward the end of the Tang Dynasty, three brothers—Wang Chao, Wang Shengui, and Wang Shenzhi—coming from Gushi, Guangzhou, Henan, ventured south to Fujian with the uprising force. By a stroke of fate, Wang Chao became the leader of the force and, with the support of the local people, took control of Quanzhou. After governing the city diligently for five years, they accumulated enough power to take control of Fuzhou in 893, eventually unifying the entire Fujian region. Quanzhou was administered by Wang Shengui, who upheld Wang Chao's governing strategies and focused on reassuring the populace, supporting agriculture, and promoting people's welfare. His son, Wang Yanbin, became renowned in history as *Zhaobao Shilang* (Minister of Summoning Treasures). Quanzhou's overseas trade grew and flourished as Wang Yanbin made an effort to develop the city. Under his rule, large merchant ships sailing overseas never sank, indicating the advanced level of shipbuilding and long-distance navigation during that time. Moreover, Quanzhou ranked first in ten kingdoms in terms of cultural relics.

其后，出身寒微的留从效主政泉州。他体察民间疾苦，进一步发展农业、海贸业，招引海外商贾到泉州投资贸易。据说，在他治下的泉州，仓库里堆满了粮食，高楼万家，城堞有数里之长。他主持扩建了城池，绕城种植刺桐树，刺桐城的名称便由此而来。继留从效之后，陈洪进主政泉州，他热衷于向宋王朝进贡从海外舶来的珍贵香料、药物，以获取朝廷对他的支持，这也刺激了民间海外贸易的发展繁荣。

当社会动乱席卷闽北、闽东一带时，泉州相对偏安一方，并在王朝更迭间实现了平稳过渡、迅速发展。

Subsequently, Liu Congxiao, who hailed from a humble background, took charge of governing Quanzhou. He understood the hardships faced by the common people and further developed agriculture and maritime trade, and made an effort to attract overseas merchants to make investment and trade in Quanzhou. It is said that under his rule, the warehouses in Quanzhou were filled with grain, tall buildings dotted the city, and the city walls stretched for several *li*. He oversaw the expansion of the city, around which he asked the planting of Erythrina trees, giving rise to the name of "Zayton City." Following Liu Congxiao, Chen Hongjin assumed governance over Quanzhou. He enthusiastically offered precious spices and medicines acquired through overseas trade to the Song court in order to gain their support, which indirectly brought prosperity to private overseas trade.

As struggles raged in the northern and eastern regions of Fujian, Quanzhou enjoyed relative tranquility. It adapted to the changing circumstances, achieving smoothly transition to the next dynasty and rapid development.

唐代，许多阿拉伯人“久闻中国之尊荣及物产之丰富”，不远万里来到这里开展商贸活动。他们在广州、泉州可以买到中国的丝绸、瓷器，在泉州、宁波可以很方便地买到来自日本、新罗的货物。“安史之乱”爆发后，割据势力粉墨登场，使陆上丝绸之路衰落，大唐帝国对外贸易重心逐渐转向海上。唐文宗曾下诏要求“节度观察使”对番客情况常加关心，除了征收下碇税（外国商船停靠中国码头所纳之税）、征收朝廷专买的禁卖品和接受外商赠送的礼品外，要让商品自由流通，让中外商人自由交易，不能再重复增加税率。唐政府还在泉州设置四个参军事，负责管理海外贸易事务。

During the Tang Dynasty, many Arabs, who had long heard of the "glory of China and its abundant products," traveled from afar to engage in commercial activities in Quanzhou. They could purchase Chinese silk and porcelain in Guangzhou and Quanzhou, while goods from Japan and Silla were readily available in Quanzhou and Ningbo. After the "Anshi Rebellion" occurred which led to the emergence of warlord factions and the disruption of the overland Silk Road, the foreign trade of the Tang Empire gradually shifted toward maritime routes. Emperor Wenzong of Tang once instructed the regional military governors to pay constant attention to the trade issues concerning foreign merchants. Apart from collecting anchorage tax (money payable for foreign merchant ships to anchor at Chinese ports), imperial monopoly goods upon which the court had imposed restrictions, and gifts presented to the court by foreign merchants, the authorities aimed to allow the free circulation of goods and promote unrestricted trade between Chinese and foreign merchants, without increasing tax rates. The Tang government also appointed four military officers in Quanzhou to take charge of overseas trade affairs.

为适应经济发展，武周久视元年（700），泉州州治由丰州迁往鲤城，唐故城有四个城门，城周 13.2 里。至唐末，王潮兄弟据泉时，在故城内建子城。留从效治泉时扩建了泉州外城，即罗城，城门由四个扩大到七个，城周增至 20 里，此外还修建了衙城。为促进海外贸易，泉州还设立了榷利院，负责海舶货物的税利，还有专门的文武官员处理相关海外贸易事务。开元寺一座方形石塔出土了一件公元 946 年的陀罗尼石经幢，上面刻有“专客务”“海路都指挥使”等字样，这便是管理海外贸易文武官员的职位，此外，还能看到“榷利院”这一机构名称。

To facilitate the development of economy, the capital of Quanzhou was relocated from Fengzhou to Licheng in the year 700. The old city of Quanzhou during the Tang Dynasty, with a perimeter of 13.2 *li*, had four city gates. Toward the end of the Tang Dynasty when Wang Brothers were in control of Quanzhou, the Inner City was built within the old city. Under the rule of Liu Congxiao, Quanzhou's outer city, *luo cheng*, was expanded. The number of city gates increased from four to seven, and the perimeter increased to twenty *li*. Besides, he built *ya cheng*, walls surrounding Quanzhou's administrative center. To promote overseas trade, Quanzhou also established "Queliyuan," an office responsible for the taxation and profits of maritime goods, and appointed special civil and military officials to handle related overseas trade affairs. In the Kaiyuan Temple, there is Stone Dharani Pillar from the year 946, unearthed from a square stone tower, which records the positions of the officials managing overseas trade, such as "Special Guest Officer" and "Commander of the Sea Routes," as well as the office name "Queliyuan."

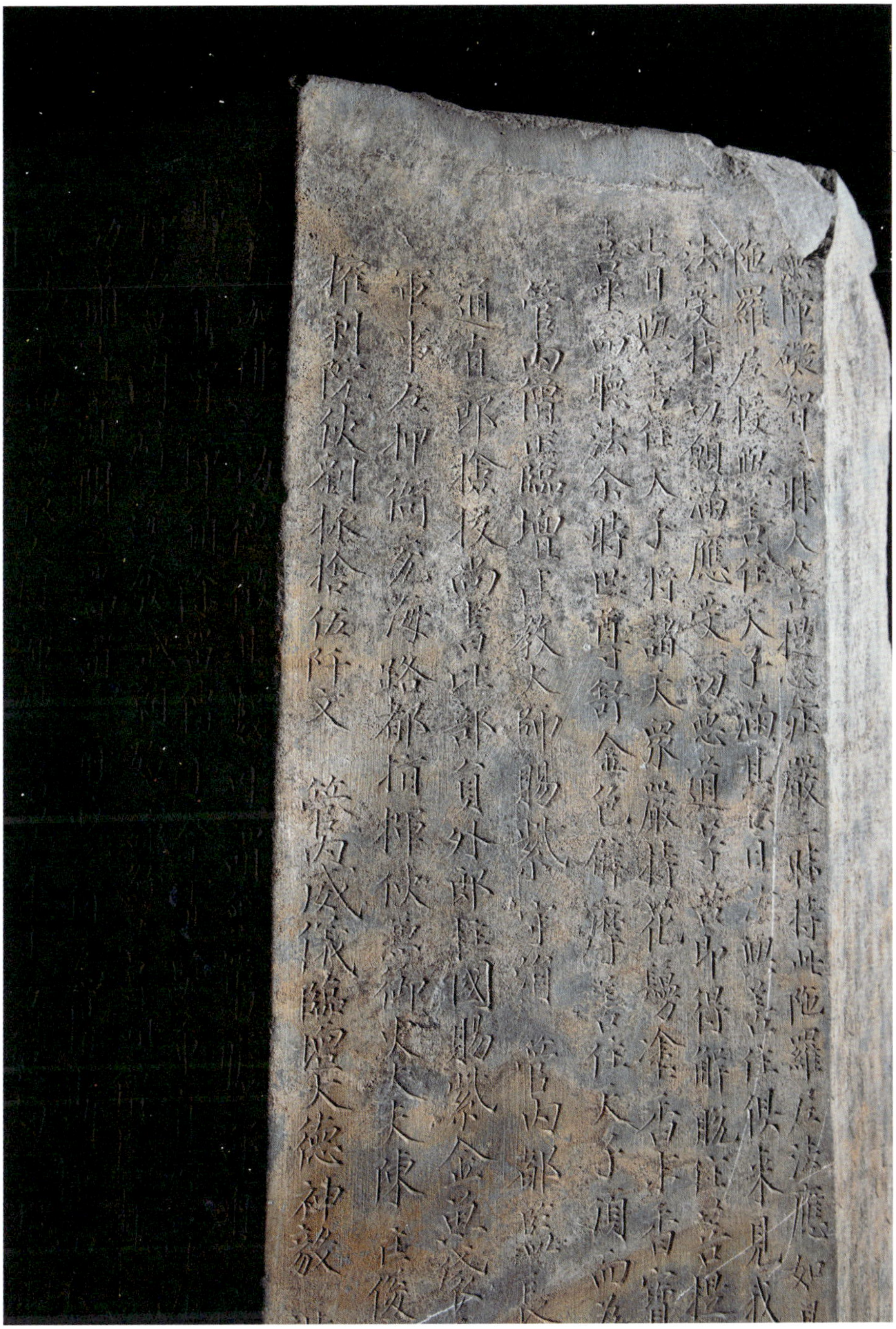

五代十国王继勋陀罗尼石经幢上“海路都指挥使”“榷利院”记载特写。（成冬冬 摄）

Close-up of the inscribed record of "Commander of the Sea Routes" and "Queliyuan" on the Stone Dharani Pillar built by Wang Jixun during the Five Dynasties and Ten Kingdoms period. (Photo by Cheng Dongdong)

唐和五代的开发使泉州逐渐兴起。唐代诗人这样描绘秋日的泉州："秋来海有幽都雁，船到城添外国人。"而冬日的泉州连年无雪，像是春天一般，正如有诗写道："连年不见雪，到处即行春。"日本船、新罗船、百济船、狮子国船、大食船、波斯舶、西域舶等海舶云集于此，来自世界各地的商人穿梭于泉州市井，贸易活动如火如荼。

唐五代的陶瓷器是重要的贸易品，美轮美奂的青瓷茶盏从泉州出海，行销世界。泉州已发现十几处唐五代的窑址，都曾是重要的青釉、青绿釉瓷器生产基地。唐代福建生产瓷器的残片曾在遥远的埃及和印度古城发现。欧洲古寺中也曾出土唐代的瓷器，都是十分珍贵的文物。

惠安山腰唐代墓葬出土的青釉二系罐。（成冬冬 摄）
A celadon jar with two lugs unearthed from an ancient tomb of the Tang Dynasty situated around the hillside in Hui'an, Quanzhou. (Photo by Cheng Dongdong)

The development during the Tang Dynasty and Five Dynasties gradually propelled Quanzhou to thrive. Poets in the Tang Dynasty depicted Quanzhou in autumn as a place where "autumn brings the arrival of distant wild geese over the sea, and ships bring foreigners to the city." There was no snow in winter, and it looked like spring, as described in the poem: "Years pass without snow; Spring springs wherever you go." The large seafaring vessels gathered here, including ships from Japan, Silla and Baekje (two ancient Korean kingdoms), Ceylon (present-day Sri Lanka but once called the Lion Country), the Arab Empire, Persia, and the Western Regions. Merchants from around the world shuttled back and forth in the Quanzhou's marketplaces, engaging in trade.

During the Tang Dynasty and Five Dynasties (618—960), ceramic wares played a significant role in trade, and exquisite celadon tea bowls were among the goods exported from Quanzhou by sea, gaining worldwide popularity. Over a dozen kiln sites from the Tang and Five Dynasties have been discovered in Quanzhou, once an important production center for celadon and bluish-green glazed porcelain. These porcelain pieces from Fujian during the Tang Dynasty were even found in distant ancient cities in Egypt and India. They have also been discovered in ancient European temples, attesting to their preciousness.

泉州的银铁冶炼业在唐五代也已经开始发展。唐人把铸铁技艺带到了婆罗洲北部（今加里曼丹岛北部），他们在那里开设铸铁厂，将铸铁技术传入东南亚。在今天的泉州还能看到一座名字很特别的寺庙——铁炉寺，它是五代治泉长官留从效的冶铁之所。泉州城内的承天寺有一处铸钱遗址，出土了钱范，这里曾是当年闽国铸造“永隆通宝”的铸币厂。

The silver and iron smelting industry had also emerged in Quanzhou during the Tang Dynasty and Five Dynasties. The Tang people brought their iron-casting techniques to the northern part of Borneo (present-day Kalimantan Island), where they established iron-casting factories and spread the technology in Southeast Asia. Quanzhou still has a unique temple today, Iron Furnace Temple, which was the iron smelting site of Liu Congxiao, an official during the Five Dynasties who governed Quanzhou. Excavations at Chengtian Temple in Quanzhou have revealed a coin casting site, where money molds were found. This was the mint where the *Yonglong Tongbao* (currency issued in the Yonglong Era in the Five Dynasties and Ten Kingdoms period) coins of the Min Kingdom were produced.

铁炉寺原址为留从效铸冶所。（吴拏云 摄）
The original site of Iron Furnace Temple was where Liu Congxiao undertook iron smelting. (Photo by Wu Nayun)

“永隆通宝”钱范 。（成冬冬 摄）
A coin mold of *Yonglong Tongbao* coins. (Photo by Cheng Dongdong)

泉州的丝织业也在唐五代时期发展起来，丝织品成为十分热门的外销商品。泉州城内的妇女们都是养蚕纺织的能手。相传，泉州人林銮从石狮的石湖港驾船前往文莱，发现那里的人们喜欢彩色的绣织品，便以“彩衣”与当地人交换香料，一往一来，利润相当可观。今天的开元寺内，一株唐代古桑依旧枝繁叶茂，它既是唐时泉州种桑养蚕历史的记录者，也是当地财主黄守恭奉献自家桑园建造佛教寺庙的见证者。

从泉州出发的商船，归来时常常货品满舱，有明珠、琉璃、香药、樟脑、蔷薇水、胡椒、肉豆蔻、龙脑等。为了稳定势力、维护关系，当时泉州的统治者可没少向上进贡这些舶来奢侈品，陈洪进在公元 976 年这一年内就向北宋朝廷连续进贡 5 次。

船是海洋贸易的载体。唐代福建所造海船，能装数千石的物品，大的海船长达 20 丈，能容纳六七百人。先进的造船技术推动了世界商贸的交流和发展。

开元寺内的千年古桑。（成冬冬 摄）
The thousand-year-old mulberry tree standing in the Kaiyuan Temple. (Photo by Cheng Dongdong)

During the Tang Dynasty and Five Dynasties, silk weaving also developed in Quanzhou, and silk products became a popular commodity for export. Women in Quanzhou were skilled in sericulture and silk weaving. Legend has it that a Quanzhou resident named Lin Luan sailed from Shihu Port in Shishi to Brunei and discovered that the local people there favored colorful embroidered fabrics. He began exchanging garments in different colors for local spices, which proved to be a profitable venture. Today, in the Kaiyuan Temple, we can still see an ancient mulberry tree from the Tang Dynasty, which not only represents the history of sericulture in Quanzhou during the Tang Dynasty but also serves as a witness to the process of a local wealthy man named Huang Shougong donating his mulberry field to build a Buddhist temple.

The merchant ships departing from Quanzhou for overseas trade often returned with loads of goods such as pearls, glassware, fragrant herbs, camphor, rose water, pepper, nutmeg, and Borneol. To maintain their influence and relationships, the rulers of Quanzhou at that time also substantially paid tribute to the Northern Song court with imported luxury goods. In the year 976, Chen Hongjin, a ruler of Quanzhou, made five consecutive tributary offerings to the Song court.

Ships were the carriers of maritime trade, and during the Tang Dynasty, the ships built in Fujian could carry thousands of *dan* (a Chinese unit of volume) of goods. The large seafaring ships were about 20 *zhang* (a Chinese unit of length. One *zhang* is equal to approximately 3.33 meters) long and could accommodate six to seven hundred people. Advanced shipbuilding technology played a crucial role in facilitating global trade and communication.

2015 年 4 月，大型舞剧《丝海梦寻》亮相联合国教科文组织总部，生动再现了泉州古港所见证的贸易往来与文化交流。（中新图片 供图）

The Dream of the Maritime Silk Road, a large-scale dance drama, performed at UNESCO headquarters in April 2015, depicting the commercial and cultural exchanges witnessed by the ancient port of Quanzhou. (Courtesy of CNSphoto.com)

宋元中国的世界港埠

China's International Port in the Song and Yuan Dynasties

海路繁荣

The Prosperous Maritime Silk Road

快速发展的宋元泉州

The Fast-Developing Quanzhou in the Song and Yuan Dynasties

为城市和海贸发展作出贡献的地方官员

Governors Who Had Contributed to the Development of the City and Maritime Trade

外国人在泉州

Foreigners in Quanzhou

艰辛的海贸历程

The Arduous Journey of Maritime Trade

丰硕的进出口货物

Abundant Imports and Exports

全社会参与的海洋贸易

Ocean Trade Involving the Entire Society

海路繁荣

经过五代时期的稳定发展，进入宋代，泉州便显示出海外贸易的强大活力。政局变化是其中一个重要因素。唐代“安史之乱”，以及北宋与辽、西夏并存，南宋与金、西夏、蒙古并立的局面，使陆上丝绸之路逐渐没落，海上丝绸之路获得了发展的契机，也给中国沿海的港口城市带来极大的利好。

蒙古的强悍最终成就了一个横跨亚欧大陆的新帝国，这进一步促进了东西方贸易的发展，原本就联通了众多国家和地区的海上丝绸之路在元朝时茁壮成长，泉州此时成为“蕃商杂处”的一个重要海上交通门户，发展达到极盛阶段。

在宋元时期世界著名旅行家的笔下，埃及的亚历山大城有四个城门，港口气势雄伟，全世界可以与它媲美的寥寥无几，中国的刺桐港便是其中一个。海上丝绸之路像是一条光彩熠熠的珠串，沿线有位于也门、常有巨型船只停泊的酷热的亚丁城；有位于伊拉克，可以通向波斯湾、印度和东亚的巴士拉，这里有从阿拉伯国家、印度、东南亚诸岛来的商人，也有中国的大船在这里装卸货物；有人们心中像伊甸园一样美丽、充满香气的锡兰岛（斯里兰卡），这里有最好的宝石和珍珠；还有位于东南亚的苏门答腊岛，黄金和樟脑等各种各样的香料琳琅满目，商人们在这里的市场或货栈里总能买到自己想要的商品。港口贸易为海上丝绸之路沿线城市创造了巨大的财富。

The Prosperous Maritime Silk Road

After a period of stable development during the Five Dynasties, Quanzhou in the Song Dynasty began to demonstrate strong vitality in overseas trade. Political changes was one of the key factors. The "Anshi Rebellion" in the Tang Dynasty, the Northern Song coexisting with the Liao (907—1125) and Western Xia (1038—1227) dynasties, and the Southern Song coexisting with the Jin (1115—1234), Western Xia, and Mongol empires, hindered the development of the overland Silk Road, but provided development opportunities for the Maritime Silk Road and brought great benefits to the coastal ports of China.

The powerful Mongol force eventually became a new empire spanning large areas of Asia and Europe, further promoting the development of East-West trade. The Maritime Silk Road, which was already connected to numerous countries and regions, continued to advance during the Yuan Dynasty (1271—1368). At this time, Quanzhou became an important maritime gateway known for being bustling with foreign merchants, reaching the height of prosperity.

According to famous travelers of the Song and Yuan dynasties, the city of Alexandria in Egypt was a magnificent port with four grand city gates, and only a few ports, including China's Zayton Port, could be on a par with it. The Maritime Silk Road was like a shining string of beads connecting many cities along the routes: there was the scorching city of Aden in Yemen, where giant ships often anchored; there was Basra in Iraq, an important port leading to the Persian Gulf, India, and East Asia, which attracted merchants from Arabia, India, and the Southeast Asian islands, and Chinese ships also anchored here to load and unload goods; there was also the beautiful and fragrant paradise-like island of Ceylon, known for its finest gemstones and pearls; there was Sumatra in Southeast Asia where merchants could always find the commodities they desired in the markets and storehouses: gold, camphor, and other spices. Port trade created immense wealth for the cities along the Maritime Silk Road.

宋元时期中国的重要港口主要有明州（今浙江宁波）、泉州和广州。北宋开宝四年（971），广州设立全国第一个专门管理海外贸易的机构——市舶司。北宋太平兴国三年（978），杭州设立两浙路市舶司，明州在其管辖范围内。北宋咸平二年（999），明州独立设置市舶司机构，附近区域人们通往日本、高丽的海船，要在明州办理出港手续，明州发展成为宋朝与日本、高丽开展外事活动的重要口岸。此后，一些来自东南亚、阿拉伯国家和波斯的商人也来往于明州，往东南亚、阿拉伯国家的海船要到广州办理出港手续，广州进口的乳香占全国各个港口进口总量的98.3%，这已完全处于垄断地位，广州甚至一度成为进贡贸易的指定口岸。泉州也一直追随着这两个国际港口城市的脚步。北宋元祐二年（1087），在泉州政府和百姓的共同努力下，福建市舶司终于在泉州设立，泉州把握住了快速发展的又一个机遇。

市舶司遗址。（陈英杰 摄）
Site of the Maritime Trade Office. (Photo by Chen Yingjie)

During the Song and Yuan dynasties, the major ports in China were Mingzhou (present-day Ningbo in Zhejiang Province), Quanzhou, and Guangzhou. In 971, Guangzhou established the first specialized institution for managing overseas trade in the country, known as the Shi Bo Si (Maritime Trade Office). In 978, Hangzhou established the Liangzhe Lu (the administrative division encompassing roughly the modern provinces of Zhejiang and southern Jiangsu, as well as the modern metropolitan Shanghai) Maritime Trade Office, which had jurisdiction over Mingzhou. In 999, Mingzhou established its own Maritime Trade Office. People from nearby regions who wanted to travel to Japan or Goryeo by sea had to go to Mingzhou to complete the procedures for leaving the port. Mingzhou developed into an important port for the Song court to conduct foreign affairs with Japan and Goryeo. Subsequently, some Southeast Asian, Arabian, and Persian traders also traveled to and from Mingzhou. For people heading toward Southeast Asia and Arabia, their ships had to go to Guangzhou to complete the customs procedures. Frankincense imported through Guangzhou accounted for 98.3% of the total imports across all ports in the country, indicating its complete monopoly. The city once even became a designated port for tribute trade. Quanzhou followed in the footsteps of these two international port cities in its development. In 1087, after continuous efforts by the Quanzhou government and the people, Fujian Maritime Trade Office was finally established in Quanzhou, providing another opportunity of rapid development for the city.

泉州为什么能后来居上，在元代成为东方第一大港，还是宋元中国的世界海洋商贸中心？除了城市自身的努力之外，还与当时的社会环境有关。北宋皇祐四年（1052），依智高发动了反抗宋朝的战争，率响应者入侵两广，围攻广州长达五十七天，以失败告终；宋元交替之际，元军三次入广，平定广州，在这段时间，百姓罹患战乱，或被驱逐掠夺，或遭遇寇盗，许多舟舶被征收用于战争……广州港遭受重创。

南宋建炎三年（1129），金兵长驱直入，所过皆焚烧一空，明州港也受到严重破坏。

相比之下，自唐至元末，泉州一直幸运躲过战火，终成宋元时期的国际巨港。来自意大利的犹太商人雅各·德安科纳于南宋时来到刺桐城后，他的意大利伙伴建议他到临安去采买货物，但他担心战火蔓延至临安，危及自己的生命和财产安全，无论如何不肯前行，只在刺桐城及周边进货。

朝天门是泉州古代七城门之一，千年来默默守护着生活在泉州的人们。（陈起拓 摄）
Chaotian Gate, one of Quanzhou's seven ancient city gates, safeguarding its residents for more than a thousand years. (Photo by Chen Qituo)

How did Quanzhou catch up with others and become the largest port in the East in the Yuan Dynasty and the emporium of the world in Song-Yuan China? Its development can be attributed not only to the city's own efforts but also to the social environment. In the year 1052, Nong Zhigao led an uprising against Song court, invading the Guangdong and Guangxi regions and besieging Guangzhou for 57 days. The uprising finally ended in failure. During the transition from the Song Dynasty to the Yuan Dynasty, Yuan forces launched three military campaigns in Guangzhou and finally pacified the city. Many civilians suffered from the ravages of war, displacement, looting, and encounters with bandits. Numerous boats and ships were conscripted for warfare, resulting in significant damage to the port of Guangzhou.

In the year 1129, the Jin forces launched a devastating invasion, burning everything in their path, and the port of Mingzhou also suffered severe destruction.

By comparison, Quanzhou was fortunate to have avoided the damage caused by war from the Tang Dynasty to the end of the Yuan Dynasty, eventually becoming an international mega-port during the Song and Yuan eras. Jacob D'Ancona, an Italian-Jewish merchant, came to Quanzhou in the Southern Song Dynasty. Although his Italian companion advised him to go to Lin'an (present-day Hangzhou in Zhejiang Province) to purchase goods, with his concerns about the warfare possibly reaching the city and the potential risks to his life and property, Jacob decided to stay in Quanzhou and its surrounding areas to do his business.

快速发展的宋元泉州

宋元泉州经历了数次飞跃，创造了持续四百多年的繁荣。北宋初年跻身全国三大海港，北宋中期赶上并超过明州，南宋初年与广州并驾齐驱，南宋末年超越广州，元代进入鼎盛时期。

北宋官方颇为重视东南地区，尤其是在与辽、金连年战乱的背景之下。北宋末年，由于金兵南侵，汴京（今河南开封）城破，徽钦二帝被掳北上。朝廷认为“东南久安，财力富盛，足以待敌”，他们口中的东南主要是江浙、福建一带。

The Fast-Developing Quanzhou in the Song and Yuan Dynasties

Quanzhou experienced several leaps and enjoyed over four hundred years of continuous prosperity during the Song and Yuan dynasties. In the early Northern Song Dynasty, it ranked among the top three seaports in the country. In the mid-Northern Song Dynasty, it caught up with and then surpassed Mingzhou. In the early Southern Song Dynasty, it stood on a par with Guangzhou, and by the end of the Southern Song Dynasty, it had overtaken Guangzhou. During the Yuan Dynasty, Quanzhou was in its heyday.

The Northern Song government attached considerable importance to the southeastern part of China, particularly in the context of continuous conflicts with the Liao and Jin dynasties. Toward the end of the Northern Song Dynasty, due to the Jin army's invasion from the north, the capital city of Bianjing (present-day Kaifeng in Henan Province) was captured, and the last two emperors, Huizong and Qinzong, were taken captive. The imperial court believed that the southeastern region, which they referred to as "Dongnan," was relatively safe and prosperous and capable of withstanding the enemy. "Dongnan" that they mentioned primarily referred to the areas of Jiangsu, Zhejiang, and Fujian.

《宋史》是这样介绍福建路的："福建路，盖古闽越之地。其地东南际海，西北多峻岭抵江。王氏窃据垂五十年，三分其地。宋初，尽复之。有银、铜、葛越之产，茶、盐、海物之饶。民安土乐业，川源浸灌，田畴膏沃，无凶年之忧。而土地迫狭，生籍繁伙；虽硗确之地，耕耨殆尽，亩直浸贵，故多田讼。其俗信鬼尚祀，重浮屠之教，与江南、二浙略同。然多向学，喜讲诵，好为文辞，登科第者尤多。"

The *History of Song* describes Fujian as follows: "Fujian Lu (an administrative division similar to Fujian Province) is the ancient land of Minyue. It is bounded by the sea to the southeast and rugged mountains to the northwest. The Wang clan illegally occupied this land for nearly fifty years. The region was divided by three forces. Then it was completely regained at the beginning of the Song Dynasty. It produces silver, copper, and *ge yue* (ramie) as well as abundant tea, salt, and marine products. People live in contentment, enjoy their work, and the fields are irrigated by rivers and springs, yielding fertile crops without concerns of famine. Yet, there were numerous land disputes that were mainly caused by a dense population with limited land—most of the land, even the relatively hard and nearly barren pieces, had been cleared for use, and the land price was rocket high. Culturally, the local customs include belief that ghosts existed, practice of worship, and embrace of Buddhism, similar to those in Jiangnan Lu and Liangzhe Lu. In addition, local residents attached great importance to education, and cultivated a love for lecture, recitation and composition, resulting in a large number of successful candidates in the imperial examinations."

这段话告诉我们几个重要信息：福建是一片沃土，长期安定；这里能开发的土地基本都开发了，相关的诉讼纠纷多；经济发展促进了人文兴盛，这里登第的人数多。

This passage provides several important pieces of information: Firstly, Fujian is a fertile land that has enjoyed long-term stability. Secondly, most of the cultivating land in the region has been developed, leading to numerous land disputes. And thirdly, economic development has fostered cultural prosperity, with a significant number of individuals achieving success in the imperial examinations.

今天的泉州德化，田野金黄，风吹稻香。（张九强 摄）

Today's Dehua, Quanzhou: scent of ripening rice wafting around the golden fields. (Photo by Zhang Jiuqiang)

南宋皇室更加依赖市舶之利，他们需要海外贸易的税收，也需要海外进口的奢侈品。南宋开国皇帝赵构认为，海外贸易的利润最为丰厚，如果实现规模发展，每年税收可达数百万贯，岂不比从普通百姓身上征税强吗？为了使这样的税收助益国家，朝廷决定遵循以前的办法，招徕他国商人来中国做生意，实现货物和财富的流通。由于泉州社会稳定、海贸利润丰腴，南宋建炎三年（1129），349 名皇室成员迁居泉州，其管理机构南外宗正司也一并随迁，至南宋绍定六年（1233），这里的皇族成员增至 2,314 人。泉州海外贸易的税收收入在一些时期已占南宋总财政收入的 2% 左右。南宋朝廷对泉州的重视与日俱增，比如，他们在官方文本中常用“泉、广市舶司”或“广、福市舶司”，把泉州与广州并列相称。这是泉州经济地位提升的印证，泉州在人们的认知中已是重要的海贸城市。

管理皇族宗室事务的南外宗正司于南宋时随迁居的宗室人员迁至泉州。（傅捷雄 摄）
The Southern Clan Office responsible for managing the affairs of the members of the imperial family who moved south and settled in Quanzhou in the Southern Song Dynasty. (Photo by Fu Jiexiong)

The Southern Song court relied more heavily on the benefits of maritime trade. The imperial court needed the tax revenue generated from overseas trade, and they had a demand for luxury goods imported from abroad. Emperor Zhao Gou, the founder of the Southern Song Dynasty, believed that overseas trade offered the most profits. If developed on a large scale, it could generate tax revenue worth millions of strings of cash each year, which would be a better source of revenue than taxing ordinary citizens. To collect this kind of tax for the country's development, the imperial court decided to follow the methods employed in the past: they welcomed foreign merchants to China for business, facilitating the circulation of goods and wealth. The social stability of Quanzhou and the abundant profits from maritime trade attracted 349 members of the Southern Song imperial family to Quanzhou in 1129. Their administrative institution, the Southern Clan Office, also moved there, and by 1233, the number of imperial family members had increased to 2,314. At certain periods, the tax revenue from Quanzhou's overseas trade accounted for approximately two percent of the Southern Song Dynasty's fiscal income. The Southern Song court attached increasingly great importance to Quanzhou. For example, in some official texts, they often used the phrase "Quan-Guang Shi Bo Si" or "Guang-Fu Shi Bo Si," placing Quanzhou on a par with Guangzhou, which confirmed the rising economic status of Quanzhou. In people's minds, Quanzhou had become an important city featuring prosperous overseas trade.

进入元朝，泉州已经形成了完整的商业城市格局、完备的港口设施、成熟的海贸传统习俗和稳定的海外联系网络，掌握了先进的造船航海技术。元政府以泉州为海贸中心，鼓励海外商人来中国贸易，实行“其往来互市，各从所欲”的开放原则，还对泉州货物进口给予一定优惠。

泉州的政治地位也日益提升，圣旨密集到来的现象可以印证这一点：元至元十九年（1282），四月发 5 道圣旨，十月发 10 道，元至元二十五年（1288）发 24 道。元至元十七年（1280），福建行省治于泉州，泉州的政治地位达到了历史最高峰。元朝整顿市舶相关条例时，要求各地市舶司在税则法规上依照泉州的办法施行。

By the Yuan Dynasty, Quanzhou had developed a complete commercial urban structure, well-established port facilities, mature maritime trade traditions and customs, a stable overseas network, and advanced shipbuilding and navigation technologies. Taking Quanzhou as a sea trade center, the Yuan government encouraged foreign traders to do business with China. They adopted an open policy toward foreign traders, allowing them to conduct trade freely according to their own preferences. Additionally, favorable policies were granted to imported goods in Quanzhou.

The increasing political status of Quanzhou can be seen from the frequent issuance of imperial edicts. In the fourth lunar month of 1282, five imperial edicts were sent to Quanzhou, followed by ten in the tenth lunar month, and 24 in 1288. In 1280 when the Fujian Xingzhongshusheng (Fujian Provincial Administration) was set in Quanzhou, Quanzhou's political status reached its historical peak. During the Yuan Dynasty's administrative reforms in maritime trade, all local Maritime Trade Offices were required to implement tax regulations according to the methods used in Quanzhou.

元奉使波斯碑，出土于泉州南校场旧址，是元代泉州发挥中外往来枢纽作用的见证。（成冬冬 摄）

The stele recording a diplomatic mission to Persia during the Yuan Dynasty, excavated from the Site of the Southern Drill Grounds in Quanzhou, bears testimony to Quanzhou as a hub building up contacts between China and the rest of the world in the Yuan Dynasty. (Photo by Cheng Dongdong)

元朝文人吴澄曾这样描述泉州："泉，七闽之都会也。番货远物，异宝珍玩之所渊薮。殊方别域，富商巨贾之所窟宅，号为天下最。"《元朝名臣事略》一书是这样描绘泉州的："民物日以繁息，仓廪之积，盈衍于外，海内翕然，号为极治。"海内外的商人与货物汇聚于此，盛大之状仿若云气腾涌。

泉州海外贸易的发展，推动了周边基础设施不断兴建和完善。宋朝海洋贸易兴盛，留下不少设施沿用至今。那时，泉州曾掀起史无前例的"造桥热"。三百多年间，泉州府所属各县共建 139 座跨江、跨海大石桥，包括洛阳桥、安平桥、石笋桥、顺济桥等，有"闽中桥梁甲天下"的美誉。桥梁建设密切了码头与城区、海港与腹地的联系，有效地促进了泉州海外贸易的发展。

Wu Cheng, a literator of the Yuan Dynasty, described Quanzhou as the "capital of the Seven Min regions." He regarded it as a place where various exotic goods and treasures were abundant, and where wealthy merchants and magnates from distant lands resided, making it the foremost destination in the world. The book *Brief Biographies of Famous Ministers of the Yuan Dynasty* records, "The population and resources are increasing daily, with granaries overflowing, and surplus spreading beyond. Throughout the realm, there is unanimous acclaim, calling it a period of perfect governance." Merchants and goods from all over the world converged on Quanzhou like surging clouds.

The development of overseas trade in Quanzhou spurred the continuous construction and improvement of surrounding infrastructure. Overseas trade in Song Dynasty prospered, and many of the facilities are still in use today. At that time, there was an unprecedented "bridge-building craze" in Quanzhou. Over a span of more than 300 years, a total of 139 large stone bridges were built across rivers and seas in the counties under the jurisdiction of Quanzhou Prefecture. These bridges included Luoyang Bridge, Anping Bridge, Shisun Bridge, and Shunji Bridge, earning Quanzhou the reputation of having "the best bridges in China." The construction of these bridges closely connected the docks with the city, and the seaport with the hinterland, effectively promoting the development of Quanzhou's overseas trade.

顺济桥遗址。（成冬冬 摄）
Site of Shunji Bridge. (Photo by Cheng Dongdong)

六胜塔、万寿塔等一系列地标建筑，在泉州城区和港口建立起来。这一时期，指南针应用于航海，让传统的地文、水文、天文导航插上了科学的翅膀，船只行驶得更远、海外贸易航线不断延伸、交流网络更加广阔。由赵彦卫撰写、成书于南宋开禧年间的《云麓漫钞》，提到了30多个与泉州有贸易往来的海外国家和地区；南宋地理学家赵汝适编撰的《诸蕃志》中记录的当时到泉州开展贸易的海外诸国增至58个；在元代地理学家汪大渊的《岛夷志略》中，记载的同泉州开展贸易往来的国家和地区已达99个。

至宋元时期，一个个码头在泉州蜿蜒的海岸拔地而起，包括外港的石湖码头、沿江的江口码头等，各自承担着不同货物的装卸和补给，海外贸易日益繁荣，刺桐港蜚声世界。位于晋江下游入海口的江面是刺桐港最繁忙的港区，这一带江面宽阔，风平浪静，为古代木帆船提供了理想的泊位，从这里溯晋江而上可抵州县，泛海可贸异邦。刺桐港对外贸易范围的不断扩大以及进出口商品的增多，不仅给这个梯航万国的港口城市带来了空前的繁荣，也使它成为东方最大的商品集散港口，被当代欧洲学者称为“世界的货舱”。

A series of landmarks for geographical navigation, such as the Liusheng Pagoda and Wanshou Pagoda, were established in Quanzhou city and port. The compass began to be used in navigation, giving traditional geographical, hydrographic, and astronomical navigation scientific wings, enabling ships to sail farther, trade routes to extend further and trade networks to become broader. *Zhao Yanwei's Historical Notes*, written around Kaixi period (1205—1207) during the Southern Song Dynasty by Zhao Yanwei, recorded trade relations between Quanzhou and over 30 overseas countries and regions. *Records of Foreign Countries* by Zhao Rukuo, a geographer in the Southern Song Dynasty, documented that the number of overseas countries trading with Quanzhou had increased to 58. Another geographer in the Yuan Dynasty, Wang Dayuan, updated that number to 99 in his book *A Brief Account of Island Inhabitants.*

During the Song and Yuan dynasties, a series of wharves were constructed along Quanzhou's winding coastline, including the Shihu Dock in the outer harbor and the Estuary Docks along the river. Each port served different purposes in terms of cargo handling and replenishment. Quanzhou's overseas trade was increasingly prosperous, and the Zayton Port had become famous around the world. The most prosperous harbor area of Zayton Port was located at the mouth of the Jinjiang River, where the river was wide without large waves. It provided the ideal berths for ancient wooden sailboats. From there, ships could sail up the Jinjiang River to reach various counties or venture into the sea to engage in trade with foreign lands. As the scope of overseas trade expanded and the volume of import and export goods increased, Zayton Port not only brought unprecedented prosperity to this international port city but also established it as the largest commercial distribution hub in the East. Contemporary European scholars have referred to it as the "world's cargo hold."

海外贸易也促进了泉州乡镇的发展，出现不少因海贸而兴盛的港镇。北宋时期推行新政，海船在泉州南部的安海港停泊、定税，官吏监税于石井津，南宋建炎四年（1130）置石井镇。安海港是泉州南部的交通要冲，这里海面辽阔，风浪小，许多货物可由此转运南安、安溪、永春一带。安海原本东边有旧市，后来西边又形成了新市，由于经商环境日盛，就将此处设为镇，市场就叫安海市，镇名为安海镇。这里当时可谓帆樯如云，商人如织，货物如山，店铺如星，吸引着四方追逐利润的商人们。

今天晋江的新街村，据说宋元时期来自阿拉伯国家和波斯的外国人常常停船于此，来往的人多了，便打造出一个新的街市，称为新街。再向外，便是南来北往的海船必然要停泊的一个海港——围头湾，它是泉州的一个重要的外港。除了云集的货船，这里还有各种各样的酒馆和店铺，数不尽的客商曾徜徉于此。离泉州城较近的港口码头也是一派繁荣景象。距泉州城仅约 10 千米的后渚港尚存两条宽三米、由花岗岩条石铺成的路，有的石板非常光滑，不知道多少宋元时期的商人、官员曾从此踏过。

Overseas trade also promoted the development of towns and villages in Quanzhou, giving rise to prosperous port towns. During the Northern Song Dynasty, the implementation of new policies allowed ships to anchor in Quanzhou's Anhai Port and then check the tax. Officials supervised taxing work at Shijing Ferry, which was upgraded to Shijing Town in 1130. Anhai Port was an important transportation hub in the southern part of Quanzhou. With the vast sea area and calm waters, many goods could be transported from here to Nan'an, Anxi, and Yongchun. Originally, there was an old market on the east side of Anhai, and later a new market formed on the west side. Due to the flourishing business environment, this area was designated as a town, and the market became known as Anhai Market, giving rise to the name Anhai Town. At that time, the town was bustling with countless sails and masts, multitudinous merchants, mountains of goods, and numerous shops, attracting businessmen from all directions in pursuit of profits.

Today in Jinjiang's Xinjie Village, it is said that during the Song and Yuan dynasties, foreigners from the Arab world and Persia often anchored their ships there. As the number of people coming and going increased, a new market was established, known as Xinjie (literally meaning "New Street"). Further out, there was Weitou Bay, a significant outer port of Quanzhou, where ships from the north and south would inevitably anchor. In addition to the flocking cargo ships, there were various taverns and shops, and countless merchants once wandered here. The ports and wharves closer to Quanzhou city also thrived. In Houzhu Port, only about ten kilometers away from Quanzhou city, there are still two roads paved with granite slabs, three meters in width. Some of the stone slabs are extremely smooth, and one can only imagine how many merchants and officials from the Song and Yuan dynasties walked on these roads.

泉州后渚港，承载着宋元时期向海而兴的故事。（成冬冬 摄）
Houzhu Port of Quanzhou: a place to tell stories of maritime prosperity during the Song and Yuan dynasties. (Photo by Cheng Dongdong)

宋元时期泉州海外贸易腾飞式发展，推动了各行各业的兴盛。在农业生产上，由于人口从几十万增长到一百多万，耕地匮乏的泉州人，把土地开垦到了极致。正如宋代安溪知县黄锐描述的那样："步丘皆力穑，掌地也成田。线引山腰路，针穿石眼泉。"为解决粮食问题，宋真宗还引进了越南的占城稻，这种水稻比较耐旱，而且生长期短。北宋初年，宋真宗考虑到福建的田地多在地势高的山上，又听闻占城稻比较耐旱，便遣使求来十石种子给人民种植。占城稻在福建地区得以推广。南宋时，很多北方人迁入泉州，他们习惯吃面食，面粉的市场需求不断扩大，物以稀为贵，小麦价格水涨船高，种植麦子所获利润达到了数倍于水稻的程度。如此高额的利润刺激了大麦和小麦的种植。与粮食种植相关的陂、塘等水利事业也日益受到官府重视，取得较大发展。

雨中插秧。（陈起拓 摄）
Planting rice seedlings in the rain. (Photo by Chen Qituo)

During the Song and Yuan dynasties, Quanzhou's overseas trade experienced a booming development, which led to the prosperity of various sectors. In terms of agricultural production, as the population grew from hundreds of thousands to over one million, the people of Quanzhou, who faced a scarcity of arable land, had cultivated the land to the utmost. As described by Huang Rui, the county magistrate of Anxi during the Song Dynasty, "Every hill is meticulously cultivated, and every inch of land becomes a field. Quanzhou people hewed out thread-like mountain paths, and dug out needle-like mountain springs." To solve the food shortage, Emperor Zhenzong of the Song Dynasty even introduced from Vietnam Champa Rice, a more drought-resistant crop with shorter time to become ripe. In the early Northern Song Dynasty, in view of the fact that plowed fields in Fujian were mostly on hills, the emperor sent envoys specifically to request ten *dan* of seeds from Champa, which later became popular in Fujian. During the Southern Song Dynasty, many people from the northern regions migrated to Quanzhou. They were accustomed to eating wheat-based foods, which resulted in a strong demand for flour in the market. The price of wheat soared due to its scarcity, and the profits from wheat cultivation were several times higher than that from rice cultivation. Such high profits stimulated some farmers to cultivate barley and wheat. Water management projects such as embankments and ponds related to crop cultivation also received increasing attention from the government and experienced significant development.

泉州造船业的规模也不断扩大。1974 年，在泉州湾后渚港曾发掘一艘南宋海船，惊艳了考古界。无论是水密隔舱精细的捻缝技术，还是出水的香料药物，都给人留下深刻的印象。中国东南沿海海岸线曲折，海道深阔，风强潮急，福船的尖底造型较好地适应了这种环境。这艘古船是典型的、成熟的福船船型，船体扁阔，底部尖削，从侧面看，斜剖面弧度非常平缓，从顶部看就像一片树叶一样漂在水面上，线型优雅流畅，有助于保持较高航速。而且，这样的船型吃水深，可以减小船只横向摇晃的幅度。

The shipbuilding in Quanzhou also developed. When the Southern Song Dynasty ship was unearthed in 1974 in Houzhu Port, Quanzhou Bay, it amazed the archaeologists. The highly sophisticated caulking technique applied to building watertight compartments, and spices as well as medicine recovered, made a strong impression on people. The ancient ship salvaged is a typical and mature type of *Fu-Chuan*. With the design of a pointed bottom, the *Fu-Chuan* adapted well to the special geographical environment, where deep and broad waterways, strong winds, and swift tides are common along the winding coastline of the southeast of China. The hull is wide and flat, with a sharply tapered bottom. When viewed from the side, the cross-section has a very gentle curve, and from the top, it resembles a leaf floating on the water. Its lines are exceptionally elegant. The graceful line design contributes to improving sailing speed. Such kind of *Fu-Chuan* boasts a deep draft, providing strong resistance to lateral drift.

1974 年泉州湾宋代海船发掘现场。（泉州海外交通史博物馆 供图）
The excavation site of Song Dynasty Oceangoing Ship at Quanzhou Bay in 1974. (Courtesy of Quanzhou Maritime Museum)

泉州宋船的出土使我们有幸一睹水密隔舱结构的奥妙。船内有 12 个隔舱板把船舱分割为 13 个舱室，隔舱板同时也增加了船的横向强度，再采用捻缝技术填补木板之间的空隙，使船板密不透水。由于各个舱室都形成相对密闭的空间，单个舱室漏水，并不会祸及其他舱室，就算少数几个舱室进水，船也不至于沉没，从而提升了远航的安全生存概率。中国最迟在唐代时便有了这种技术，欧洲国家 18 世纪时从中国学会这门技术。宋人能打造出性能优良的远洋福船，与泉州长久以来积累的航海、造船经验息息相关。当时，泉州所造海船远近闻名，甚至宋人的老对手金人也请福建人打造战船。

The excavation of the Song Dynasty ship in Quanzhou Bay has given us the privilege to witness the awe-inspiring watertight bulkheads. The ship had 12 bulkheads that divided the hull into 13 compartments. These bulkheads increased the lateral strength of the ship, and the employed caulking technique to fill the gaps between the wooden planks made the ship watertight. Due to the relatively sealed nature of each compartment, even if one compartment leaked, it would not affect the other compartments, and even if a few compartments took on water, the ship would not sink, thus increasing the probability of survival during long-distance voyages. China had already developed this technology as early as the Tang Dynasty, while Europe only learned it from China in the 18th century. The ability to construct high-performance oceangoing *Fu-Chuan* during the Song Dynasty was closely related to Quanzhou's long-standing maritime and shipbuilding experience. At that time, Quanzhou's reputation for shipbuilding spread far and wide, to the extent that even the Song's adversary, the Jin people, sought the assistance of Fujian people in constructing warships.

泉州湾宋代海船隔舱板结构。（成冬冬 摄）
The structure of the bulkheads between compartments in the Song Dynasty Oceangoing Ship at Quanzhou Bay. (Photo by Cheng Dongdong)

福船水密隔舱内部结构展示模型。（段燕飞 摄）
Demonstration model of the interior structure of watertight bulkheads in *Fu-Chuan*. (Photo by Duan Yanfei)

收藏在泉州湾古船陈列馆里的泉州湾宋代海船。（陈起拓 摄）
The Song Dynasty Oceangoing Ship at Quanzhou Bay on display in the Exhibition Hall of Ancient Ship in Quanzhou Bay. (Photo by Chen Qituo)

泉州的纺织业、陶瓷业、冶炼业、制糖业等行业也都在海外贸易快速发展的环境下逐渐壮大。泉州出产的丝织品有缎、绢、罗等，外销东亚、东南亚、南亚、西亚、非洲等地的 70 多个国家。从宋元时期窑址出土的陶瓷器，包括军持、小口瓶、碗、钵、缸、盘、碟、罐等日用品，黑釉、白釉、青釉一应俱全，直至今天还能在世界各地追寻到它们的踪迹。冶炼铸造业在宋元时期也超越前代，其中冶铁业最为发达。泉州境内许多丘陵和山地铁矿丰富，古矿洞和铁渣遍布安溪、永春、德化、晋江、惠安等地的丘陵，安溪冶铁最为知名，经考古调查，发现安溪青阳下草埔冶铁遗址是宋代中国第一个铸造块炼铁的冶铁场所。

Various industries in Quanzhou, such as textiles, ceramics, metallurgy, and sugar refining, also grew gradually as overseas trade was undergoing rapid development. Quanzhou produced a wide range of silk fabrics, including satin, chiffon, gauze, and other products. These products were exported to over 70 countries in East Asia, Southeast Asia, South Asia, West Asia, Africa, and other regions. The ceramic wares from the Song and Yuan kiln sites, including kendis (portable vessels used for holding water and washing hands), small-mouth bottles, bowls, basins, vats, plates, dishes, and jars for daily use, featured black, white, and celadon glazes, and their traces can still be found in various parts of the world today. Metallurgy and casting also surpassed the previous eras during the Song and Yuan dynasties, with iron smelting being particularly advanced. Quanzhou was rich in iron ore deposits in many hilly areas, and the remnants of mines and iron slag can be found throughout Anxi, Yongchun, Dehua, Jinjiang, Hui'an, and other hilly regions. Among them, Anxi's iron smelting was particularly well-known. Archaeological discoveries revealed that the Xiacaopu Iron Production Site of Qingyang Village in Anxi was the first iron smelting site in China during the Song Dynasty to forge sponge iron.

收藏在泉州海外交通史博物馆内的宋代褐色牡丹芙蓉纹罗残片。（成冬冬 摄）

A brown silk scrap with peony and hibiscus pattern from the Song Dynasty in Quanzhou Maritime Museum. (Photo by Cheng Dongdong)

磁灶窑黑釉剔花双耳炉。（成冬冬 摄）

A black-glazed and double-eared pot incised with floral pattern from Cizao Kilns. (Photo by Cheng Dongdong)

为城市和海贸发展作出贡献的地方官员

泉州繁荣的海外贸易和多元和谐的城市格局，离不开官方的支持。南宋初期，大批皇室成员迁入泉州，经数代繁衍生息，至南宋末期，人数已达三千多人。他们作为重要的政治力量，广泛参与社会治理和其他各项事务，如兴建安平桥、组织祈风典礼等，并积极开展海外贸易，极大地刺激了高端消费市场，进一步促进了泉州的发展繁荣。北宋时期，没有一位皇室宗亲担任过泉州市舶长官，而从南外宗正司迁入泉州到南宋灭亡的一百多年间，共有 11 位成员担任过泉州市舶使一职，占该职位任职人数的十分之一。这强化了国家政权对泉州海洋贸易的推动，成为强有力的官方管理保障。

Governors Who Had Contributed to the Development of the City and Maritime Trade

The prosperous overseas trade and diverse but harmonious landscape of Quanzhou owed much to the involvement of the government. In the early Southern Song Dynasty, lots of members of imperial family moved to Quanzhou, and over several generations, its population grew to over 3,000 people by the end of the Southern Song Dynasty. As an important political force, the Southern Clan actively participated in social governance and other various affairs such as the construction of Anping Bridge, organizing wind-praying ceremonies, and actively engaging in overseas trade. Their activities greatly stimulated high-end consumer market, further promoting the development and prosperity of the city. During the Northern Song Dynasty, no members of the imperial clan served as Superintendent of Maritime Trade Office. However, from the time the Southern Clan Office relocated to Quanzhou until the fall of the Southern Song Dynasty, 11 imperial clan members held that position, accounting for one-tenth of the total, which strengthened the government's promotion of maritime trade in the city and reflected robust official management and support.

南宋淳熙十年（1183）冬季遣舶祈风石刻。（成冬冬 摄）

The stone inscription of wind praying for a smooth sea voyage in winter in 1183. (Photo by Cheng Dongdong)

南宋乾道七年（1171），汪大猷任泉州知州。那时，常有海贼在海滨地区抢掠，干扰粮米、货品的正常运输，农业和商业活动都受到影响。汪大猷任职期间，命人在这里建造两百间房屋，派遣约一千名将士长期屯戍于此，保护居民正常开展农业生产和商业活动，维护了国防，也保证了海上航线的正常运行。同时，对来泉的外国商人以礼相待，维护泉州港国际海贸的顺利开展。在处理与外商相关的案件时，改变了过往番汉之间发生冲突后采用的以牛抵罪的外国习俗，一律采用中国律法处置。这既维护了古代中国法治尊严，又为港口城市的良性发展提供了法治保障。汪大猷还废弃了为供应宗室而苛剥百姓的做法。他裁减政府开支、采购广东粮米，并清理隐田租给农民，调剂了民需、军需和宗室粮食供应，稳定了社会秩序。

In 1171, Wang Dayou served as the governor of Quanzhou. At that time, the coastal areas were frequently plagued by pirates, which disrupted the normal transportation of grain and goods. It caused disturbances in agricultural and commercial activities. During Wang Dayou's tenure in Quanzhou, he ordered the construction of 200 houses and stationed around 1,000 soldiers here for a long period. This protected the normal agricultural production and business activities, maintained national defense, and ensured the smooth operation of maritime routes. Additionally, foreign merchants were treated with courtesy, so that the international maritime trade in Quanzhou Port could develop more smoothly. In dealing with cases involving foreign merchants, he changed the previous foreign custom of using cattle to atone when disputes between the foreigners and Han people arose, and instead applied Chinese laws uniformly. This not only upheld the dignity of ancient Chinese legal governance but also provided legal protection for the sound development of the port city. Wang Dayou also abolished the practice of excessively taxing the common people to support the imperial family. He reduced government expenditures, purchased grain from Guangdong, and reorganized unregistered fields to rent them to farmers. This adjustment addressed issues related to civilian and military needs, as well as the food supply for the imperial family, thereby stabilizing social order.

"涨海声中万国商"场景再现。（段燕飞 摄）

A scene replication of "Merchants from All Nations Thronging to Quanzhou Amidst the Sound of Rising Tides." (Photo by Duan Yanfei)

南宋嘉定十年(1217)和绍定五年(1232),真德秀两次出任泉州知州。当时，泉州的吏治和社会环境都不乐观，海贸也趋于凋敝。真德秀上任后便着手整顿吏治、选贤任能。由于泉州宝货如山，许多官员受到诱惑，以“和买”的名义刮取商人货品和利润，导致从泉州港征收的税赋降低了一半多，也使外国的海船骤减。真德秀坚决打击贪官污吏，抄没贪腐官员的财产充公。他常常劝勉同僚要“律己以廉，抚民以仁，存心以公，莅事以勤”。吏治优良是海贸发展繁荣的基础。真德秀与市舶司的赵崇度一同革除积弊，罢除“和买”，经过数年努力，终于使来往于泉州港的海舶从每年几艘恢复到每年三十多艘，国家的税赋也随之增长。真德秀还严厉打击地主盘剥，调动农民的生产积极性，采取措施加固海防，从而维护社会稳定，恢复泉州港的海外贸易。深受百姓爱戴的真德秀，留下了“海神亦叹公清德”的美名。

“真文忠公祠”石刻。(成冬冬 摄)
The stone inscription of "Zhen Wen Zhong Gong Ci" in memory of Zhen Dexiu. (Photo by Cheng Dongdong)

Zhen Dexiu served as the governor of Quanzhou twice, in the years 1217 and 1232. At that time, the governance and social environment of Quanzhou were unfavorable, and maritime trade had declined. After Zhen Dexiu took office, he started the rectification of governance and the selection of capable officials. Due to the abundance of valuable goods, many officials were tempted to engage in corrupt practices in the name of *he mai* (buying goods from merchants at low prices for personal gain) to extort profits from merchants. As a result, the tax revenue collected from Quanzhou Port had decreased by more than a half, and the number of foreign ships visiting the port significantly decreased. Zhen Dexiu took a firm stance against corrupt officials, confiscating the properties of corrupt individuals. He often reminded officials to be clean and honest, to be lenient with people, to act with fairness, and to perform duties with diligence. Healthy governance was the foundation for developing maritime trade. Together with Zhao Chongdu of the Maritime Trade Office, Zhen Dexiu abolished age-old evil practices and eliminated the *he mai* system. After several years of effort, the port, which had only a few ships annually, gradually recovered to host over thirty ships, and the country's tax revenue increased accordingly. Zhen Dexiu was also actively engaged in stopping landlords from exploiting people, encouraging farmers to improve agricultural production, and strengthening coastal defense. These efforts helped maintain social stability and revive overseas trade at Quanzhou Port. Zhen Dexiu, who was highly respected by people, left behind a good reputation, and "even a sea god would be impressed by his integrity and virtues."

元至元十三年（1276），阿拉伯人后裔蒲寿庚为保家族利益携城投降元朝，却也意外地推动了泉州经济的发展，刺桐港免遭战火，在元代达到极盛。在元代得到重用的蒲寿庚不遗余力招揽海外商人到泉州开展贸易活动，其家族曾经居住过的占城和印度南部的马八儿国商人到中国开展贸易，其他国家也纷纷效仿，与泉州通商，泉州的海外贸易极速向前发展。后来，元统治者采纳蒲寿庚的建议，沿袭宋制在泉州设立了元代第一个管理海外贸易的机构，此外，“制封泉州神女号护国明著灵惠协正善庆显济天妃”。妈祖神格升高，愈发受人尊崇，逐渐成为跨洋越海的世界性的保护神。

In 1276, Pu Shougeng, an Arab descendant, surrendered the city to the Yuan court in order to protect his family's interests. However, this event unexpectedly propelled the economic development of Quanzhou and led to the peak of its prosperity during the Yuan Dynasty, as Zayton Port was safe from wars. Pu Shougeng, who was put in an important position by Yuan court, spared no effort to attract overseas merchants to Quanzhou to do business. He facilitated trade between Quanzhou and Champa, where his family previously lived, and the Malabar in southern India. Subsequently, other countries followed suit and established trade relations with Quanzhou, resulting in rapid growth in its overseas trade. Afterward, the Yuan ruler accepted Pu Shougeng's suggestion and established the first institution for managing overseas trade in Quanzhou of the Yuan Dynasty, following the model of the Song Dynasty. Additionally, the emperor bestowed the title of "Protective Goddess of the Nation, Manifestation of Divine Grace, Co-Rectifier of Goodness, Auspiciousness, and Help" upon the deity Mazu in Quanzhou. Mazu's status was, therefore, raised. She was increasingly revered and became a world-renowned protector, crossing oceans and continents.

泉州市舶司遗址出土的“舶亭蒲□”铭文砖。（王俊 摄）

The inscribed brick of "Bo Ting Pu (?)" excavated on the Site of the Maritime Trade Office. (Photo by Wang Jun)

供奉着妈祖的天后宫。（陈英杰 摄）

Tianhou Temple dedicated to Mazu, the sea goddess. (Photo by Chen Yingjie)

元至正九年（1349），新疆人偰玉立出任泉州路达鲁花赤（元朝地方官名）。为应对盗贼四起的局面，偰玉立对罗城进行大规模的扩建，与南宋所筑翼城合，保护居民不受骚扰，新罗城的周长达到30里。“合全城观之，状如鲤”，奠定了泉州城今后几百年的规模。偰玉立治泉州期间注重营造宽松和谐的文化氛围，打造多元兼容的格局。偰玉立出身于摩尼教世家，但他本人却不信奉此教。他曾在九日山题刻“泉南佛国”，后人评价此四字“落墨古朴，自见骨力”。泉州清净寺曾经历“废坏不治”的情况，寺庙的房产和财物被人侵占，教徒曾多次控告，问题却得不到解决。偰玉立虽不信奉该教，但公正、得当地处理了该寺问题，使“是寺一新”，民心欢悦。清净寺是宋元中国与阿拉伯国家通商互动的友谊见证。偰玉立还劝人向学，重视教化，主持重修了泉州府文庙的明伦、议道二堂和斋舍、先贤祠等。人们称其为“温陵贤守”，为其建立了祠堂。

元至正十年（1350）偰玉立题“泉南佛国”。（成冬冬 摄）
The inscription of "Quan Nan Fo Guo" by Xie Yuli in 1350. (Photo by Cheng Dongdong)

In 1349, Xie Yuli from Xinjiang was appointed as Quanzhou Darughachi (a local official in the Yuan Dynasty). To address the rampant banditry in the region, Xie Yuli expanded *luo cheng* to connect it with *yi cheng* built in the Southern Song Dynasty, to protect the residents from being harassed. The perimeter of the city increased to 30 *li*. The overall shape of the city resembled a carp, laying the foundation for its size for the following centuries. During Xie Yuli's governance of Quanzhou, he attached great importance to fostering a tolerant and harmonious cultural atmosphere to promote the diversity and inclusiveness of society. Although he came from a Manichaean family, Xie Yuli himself did not embrace this religion. He had once inscribed the phrase "Quan Nan Fo Guo" (literally meaning Quanzhou as a land of Buddhism) on stone tablets in Jiuri Mountain, and his engraved calligraphy is admired by later generations for its "simplicity of strokes bearing bony strength." When the Qingjing Mosque in Quanzhou fell into disrepair and was subject to encroachment and misappropriation of its property, believers made various accusations but failed to resolve the issue. Although a non-follower of Islam, Xie Yuli impartially and appropriately addressed the problems of the mosque, leading to its restoration and bringing joy to the people. The mosque, known as Qingjing Mosque, is a witness to the friendship and trade relationship between China and the Arab world during the Song and Yuan dynasties. Xie Yuli also emphasized the pursuit of knowledge and the importance of education. He oversaw the restoration of the Minglun and Yidao halls, as well as the dormitories and the Ancestral Shrine of Sages in the Confucius Temple and School. People referred to him as "Wenling's Virtuous Guardian" and established a shrine in his honor.

外国人在泉州

泉州海外贸易的发达，吸引了来自波斯、印度、锡兰、意大利，乃至非洲一些国家的人士在此汇聚，有贵族、长老、将领、官员、宗教领袖，也有普通商人和工匠，形成了“市井十洲人”的开放包容格局。泉州成为世界商品的集散地、各国人士汇聚的舞台、各种文明交融的平台，以及技艺传播的港湾。

番客在泉州受到善待，这也是宋元政府高度重视海外贸易的体现。北宋熙宁年间，高丽人崔举航行时遭遇大风，漂流到泉州，当地渔民救了他。泉州地方政府给他发放了路条和生活费，专门派人护送他和其他一些人到明州，以便他们搭船回家。南宋绍兴年间，阿拉伯商人蒲罗辛运香料来泉州开展贸易，泉州市舶司从他的货物中抽解了价值三十万贯的货物。鉴于他对商贸的巨大贡献，朝廷授予他“承信郎”的官位。这些善待举动，鼓舞了番客，也推动了贸易。

宋代“承信郎”碑刻。（成冬冬 摄）
The inscription of "Cheng Xin Lang" during the Song Dynasty. (Photo by Cheng Dongdong)

Foreigners in Quanzhou

The prosperous overseas trade in Quanzhou attracted people from various countries such as Persia, India, Ceylon, Italy, and even some African nations, who converged here. Among them were nobles, elders, generals, officials, religious leaders, as well as ordinary merchants and craftsmen, forming an open and inclusive atmosphere known as the "Gathering of people from ten nations" in the city. Quanzhou became a hub for world commodities, a stage where people from different countries gathered, a platform for the blending of various civilizations, and a harbor for the dissemination of skills and craftsmanship.

Foreign guests, locally called *fan ke*, were treated well in Quanzhou, which reflected that the government had placed emphasis on overseas trade during the Song-Yuan period. In the Xining period (1068—1077) of the Northern Song Dynasty, a man from Goryeo named Cui Ju was caught in strong winds at sea and drifted to Quanzhou, where he was saved by local fishermen. The Quanzhou local government not only provided him with travel permits and covered his living expenses, but also sent people to accompany him and some others to Mingzhou, where they could board a ship to return home. During the Shaoxing period (1131—1162) of the Southern Song Dynasty, an Arab merchant named Pu Luoxin came to Quanzhou with valuable spices for trade. The Quanzhou Maritime Trade Office took a portion of his cargo, worth 300,000 *guan* (a Chinese unit of currency. One *guan* is a string of 1,000 coins) as tariffs. In recognition of his significant contributions to trade, the authorities granted him the official title of "Chengxin Lang." All these acts of kindness motivated foreign merchants and encouraged trade.

宋代“承信郎”碑刻拓片。（成冬冬 摄）
The rubbing of the inscription of "Cheng Xin Lang" during the Song Dynasty. (Photo by Cheng Dongdong)

来到泉州的番客们，可以保留本族习俗。他们聚居城南蕃人巷，“东起青龙聚宝、经一桥市，西至富美与风炉埕，北从横巷起，南抵聚宝街以南的宝海庵止”。这里靠近晋江，一派繁忙之景，仓库、住所、私家花园、寺庙各安其所。与番客有关的日常事务，由朝廷任命的番长进行管理。番长的职位不可世袭，德高望重的番客方可担任。穿着大宋官服的番长们穿行于熙来攘往的闹市，何尝不是一幅美妙的融合画面呢？

不同国家、不同民族的文化在泉州受到尊重。被罗马天主教教皇派往泉州的主教安德烈・佩鲁贾说：“在此大帝国境内，确有天下各国和各宗教派别之人。所有的人皆可按照各自教派而生活。”建立寺庙说明某一群体已有较多人数，也足见聚居群体对居住地的重视。泉州的外国寺庙有很多，每个信仰群体都有自己的活动场所。

The foreign guests living in Quanzhou were allowed to retain their unique customs. They gathered in an area called Fanren Lane (literally meaning "foreigners' lane") to the south of the city. "The lane covered the area that began from Qinglong and Jubao in the east all the way through Yiqiao Market to Fumei and Fenglu Cheng in the west, and from Hengxiang Lane in the north to the southern end of Jubao Street at Baohai Temple." This area was close to Jinjiang River and was bustling with activity. It had warehouses, residences, private gardens, and temples, each with a role to play. The daily affairs related to the foreign merchants were managed by *fan zhang*, or head of foreigners, appointed by the government. The position of *fan zhang* was not hereditary; only respected and esteemed foreign merchants were qualified to hold this position. They would wear official attire of the Song Dynasty as they moved through the busy market. What a splendid and harmonious scene of cultural integration!

In Quanzhou, the cultures of different countries and ethnic groups were respected. The bishop, Andrew of Perugia, sent by the Roman Catholic Pope to Quanzhou, remarked, "Within this great empire are people from various countries and religious groups, who can live by their respective beliefs." The establishment of temples indicated that certain communities had gathered a sufficient number of people and they put emphasis on their place of residence. Quanzhou was home to many foreign temples. Each faith community had its own place of gathering.

元伊斯兰教“蕃客墓”石刻。（成冬冬 摄）

The stone inscription of "Fan Ke Mu" indicating a foreigner's tomb for the religion of Islam during the Yuan Dynasty. (Photo by Cheng Dongdong)

北宋雍熙年间，天竺僧人罗护那漂洋过海来到泉州，凭借他的修行与威望，很多番商向他捐赠金子、丝织品及各色珍宝。他在泉州城南择地建造了宝林院，这是外国僧人在泉州建造的唯一一座佛教寺院。据说今天泉州大桥北侧的宝海庵正是当初的宝林院。元皇庆年间，波斯人夏不鲁罕丁跟随贡使来到泉州，住在排铺街，担任清真寺住持。他的后代也留在泉州，以“夏”为家姓。元代，一位亚美尼亚妇人捐资建造了一座雄伟华丽的天主教堂，后来成为这里天主教的总教堂……佛教、伊斯兰教、景教、天主教、摩尼教、印度教等宗教信徒都在泉州定居，泉州也因此素有“世界宗教博物馆”之称。

元印度教四角斗拱莲花石柱头。（成冬冬 摄）
Hindu lotus-shaped quadrangular *dou gong* pillar capstone of the Yuan Dynasty. (Photo by Cheng Dongdong)

During the Yongxi period (984—987) of the Northern Song Dynasty, the monk Rahula from Tianzhu arrived in Quanzhou by sea. Due to his spiritual practice and reputation, many foreign merchants donated gold, silk fabrics, and precious treasures to him. He selected a location in the southern part of Quanzhou and built the Baolin Temple, the only Buddhist temple constructed by a foreign monk in the city. It is said that the Baohai Temple to the north of Quanzhou Bridge today was the original site of Baolin Temple. During the Huangqing period (1312—1313) of the Yuan Dynasty, a respected Persian named Burhaneddin followed the tribute mission to Quanzhou and settled in the Paipu Street area, where he served as the Imam of a mosque. His posterity stayed in Quanzhou and adopted the surname "Xia." During the Yuan Dynasty, an Armenian woman donated funds to build a magnificent and splendid Catholic church, which later became the main cathedral of Catholicism in Quanzhou. Buddhism, Islam, Nestorian Christianity, Roman Catholicism, Manichaeism, Hinduism, and other religions all found a place in Quanzhou, earning the city the title of "World Museum of Religions."

宋元泉州的富庶、多元和包容，使之成为外国人眼里增长见识、躲避离乱的美好港湾。据《岛夷志略》记载，三岛一男子曾搭乘海船来泉州做生意，“罄其资囊，以文其身”。回国后，人们“以尊长之礼待之”，请他坐上座，即便长辈也不与他相争。元朝时，马八儿国宰相不阿里（也作孛哈里），经常为元朝使臣提供便利，为他们提供与伊儿汗国之间的海上交通帮助，还不断遣使至元朝通好，也曾到过中国，对元朝的海外交通作出不少贡献。后与马八儿国国王生隙，担心自己与家人受到迫害，于是投靠元朝，定居泉州。元朝皇帝给予他礼遇，他去世后，朝廷命人将其遗体从元大都送回泉州安葬，可谓善始善终。

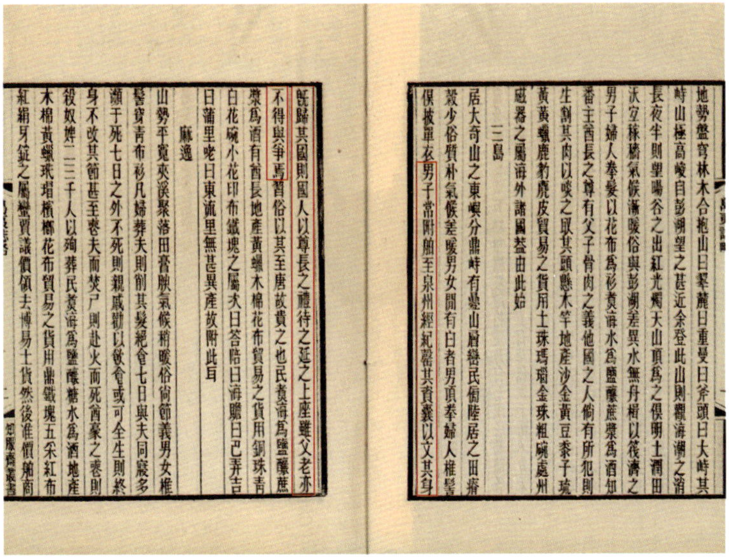
地勢盤穹林木合抱山曰翠麓曰重曼曰斧頭曰大峙其
峙山極高峻自彭湖望之甚近余登此山則觀海潮之消
長夜半則望暘谷之出紅光燭天山頂為之俱明土潤田
沃宜稼穡氣候漸暖俗與彭湖差異水無舟楫以筏濟之
男子婦人拳髮以花布為衫煮海水為鹽釀蔗漿為酒知
番主酋長之尊有父子骨肉之義他國之人倘有所犯則
生割其肉以啖之取其頭懸木竿地產沙金黃豆黍子琉
黃黃蠟鹿豹麂皮貿易之貨用土珠瑪瑙金珠粗碗處州
磁器之屬海外諸國蓋由此始

三島

居大奇山之東嶼分鼎峙有疊山層巒民傍陸居之田瘠
穀少俗質朴氣候差暖男女間有白者男頂拳婦人椎髻
俱披單衣男子常附舶至泉州經紀罄其資囊以文其身
既歸其國則國人以尊長之禮待之延之上座雖父老亦
不得與爭焉習俗以其至唐故貴之也民煮海為鹽釀蔗
漿為酒有酋長地產黃蠟木棉花布貿易之貨用銅珠青
白花碗小花印布鐵塊之屬次曰答陪曰海贍曰巴弄吉
曰蒲里咾曰東流里無甚異產故附此耳

麻逸

山勢平寬夾溪聚落田膏腴氣候稍暖俗尚節義男女椎
髻穿青布衫凡婦葬夫則削其髮絕食七日與夫同寢多
瀕于死七日之外不死則親戚勸以飲食或可全生則終
身不改其節甚至喪夫而焚尸則赴火而死酋豪之喪則
殺奴婢二三千人以殉葬民煮海為鹽釀糖水為酒地產
木棉黃蠟玳瑁檳榔花布貿易之貨用鼎鐵塊五采紅布
紅絹牙錠之屬蠻賈議價領去博易土貨然後准價掄商

《岛夷志略》中关于三岛男子在泉州文身的记载。（林瀚 供图）
The record in *A Brief Account of Island Inhabitants* about a male resident from the Philippines having tattoos done in Quanzhou. (Courtesy of Lin Han)

During the Song and Yuan dynasties, Quanzhou was known for its prosperity, diversity, and inclusiveness, making it an excellent harbor that impressed foreigners as a desirable place to broaden their horizons and seeking refuge from chaos. According to the records in the *A Brief Account of Island Inhabitants*, there was a man from the Philippines who came to Quanzhou for business. He spent all his wealth to get a tattoo while he was there. When he returned to his homeland, people treated him with great respect, offering him a seat above even the elder members of the community. During the Yuan Dynasty, there was a prominent minister in the Malabar Kingdom named Behari (also known as Bohari) who treated envoys from the Yuan court well and consistently facilitated the maritime transportation between the Yuan court and the Ilkhanate. He also sent missions to the Yuan court to strengthen friendly relations and visited China in person, contributing significantly to the overseas communication of the Yuan Dynasty. However, he fell out of favor with the king of the Malabar Kingdom. He sought refuge in the Yuan court and settled in Quanzhou, for fear that he and his family might be persecuted. The Yuan emperor treated him with courtesy. Upon his death, the Yuan court ordered his body to be sent back to Quanzhou from Dadu (the Yuan capital) for burial, which can be considered a fitting end to his life.

宋元泉州还是重要的商品制造基地，拥有先进的技术与经验，吸引了不同国家的人前来学艺交流。南宋嘉定十六年（1223），日本人加藤四郎随禅僧来到中国，学习陶瓷烧造技术，泉州德化窑是他学习的重要一站。归国后，他在日本山田郡濑户村试烧成功，并修建窑厂批量烧制陶瓷，被称为“濑户烧”，加藤四郎也被尊为日本“陶祖”。精通制糖的埃及人曾向永春人传授精制食糖的方法，永春人学会了加木灰方法制造黑砂糖的工艺，使永春产糖的数量和质量都得到提升。

曾经在宋元泉州生活或停留过的外国人，留下了许许多多关于泉州的记忆。城中的建筑、碑刻上残存的造像、符号、文字等，至今仍生动地讲述着他们曾经的故事。开元寺西塔上“唵嘛呢叭咪吽”的佛教六字真言、中国现存最早的伊斯兰教寺、因马可·波罗而得名的马可巷和马可井……它们都是泉州开放包容格局的见证。璀璨的异域文化，构成了泉州作为宋元中国的世界海洋商贸中心独特的文化魅力。

During the Song and Yuan dynasties, Quanzhou was indeed an important manufacturing base for commodities, possessing advanced technology and expertise that attracted people from different countries to come and learn and exchange skills. In the year 1223, a Japanese man named Shiro Kato came to China with a Zen monk to learn ceramics firing techniques. Quanzhou's Dehua Kilns were an important destination for his studies. After returning to Japan, he successfully conducted trial firings in Seto Village, Yamada County and established a kiln to produce ceramics in large quantities. These ceramics became known as "Seto-yaki" in Japan, and Shiro Kato was honored with the title "the founder of Seto ware pottery" in Japan. During the Yuan Dynasty, Egyptians who were highly skilled in sugar-making taught the people of Yongchun the art of sugar-making. As a result, the people of Yongchun learned the technique of making brown sugar using the "addition of wood ash" method, which significantly increased both the quantity and quality of sugar production in Yongchun.

Many foreigners who once lived or stayed in Quanzhou during the Song and Yuan dynasties left behind numerous memories about Quanzhou. The city's buildings and engraved stone tablets still bear the sculptures, symbols and inscriptions that clearly tell us what they had experienced. For instance, on the western pagoda of the Kaiyuan Temple, there are the six syllables of the Buddhist mantra "Om Mani Padme Hum." Besides, the present-day Qingjing Mosque, the earliest extant Islamic mosque ever constructed in China, Marco Lane and Marco Well, both named after Marco Polo, all serve as a testament to Quanzhou's openness and inclusiveness. Splendid exotic cultures contributed to the unique cultural charm of Quanzhou, emporium of the world in Song-Yuan China.

德化窑白瓷卷草纹盒。（成冬冬 摄）
A white porcelain box with wavy grass pattern produced in Dehua Kilns. (Photo by Cheng Dongdong)

德化窑青白釉高足杯。（成冬冬 摄）
A bluish-white glazed stem cup produced in Dehua Kilns. (Photo by Cheng Dongdong)

艰辛的海贸历程

宋元时期，泉州成为世界海洋商贸中心，雅各曾这样描述他初到刺桐港的情景：“就在我们抵达的那天，江面上至少有 15,000 艘船，有的来自阿拉伯，有的来自大印度，有的来自锡兰，有的来自小爪哇……以及来自我们国家的和来自法兰克其他王国的船只。”泉州与诸多国家和地区通商贸易，呈现“涨海声中万国商”的繁荣景象。然而繁荣背后的艰辛却少为人知。

印度尼西亚的一个岛屿叫文老古，这里的人们每年都盼望着有中国商船来这里开展贸易。当地养了一种五梅鸡，大家认为五梅鸡的出生是唐船到来的预兆：当有一只鸡雏破壳而出时，必定有一艘唐船到来；当第二只鸡雏破壳而出时，必定有第二艘唐船到来。朴实的故事，让我们看到了商船到来的不易，也看到了当地人对与中国通商的期盼。

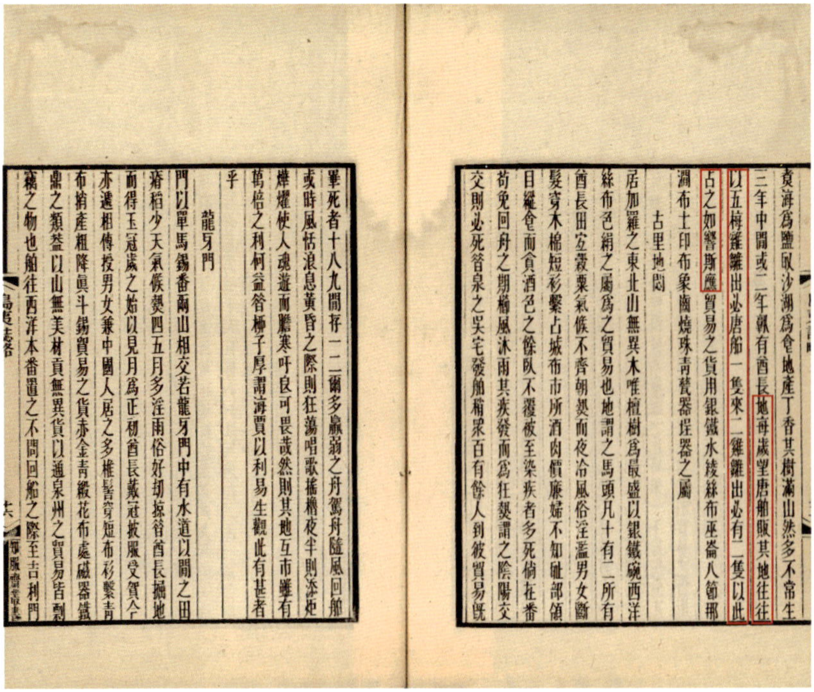

《岛夷志略》中关于文老古人盼望与中国通商的记载。（林瀚 供图）

The descriptions in *A Brief Account of Island Inhabitants* about residents in Wenlaogu eager to trade with China. (Courtesy of Lin Han)

The Arduous Journey of Maritime Trade

During the Song-Yuan period, Quanzhou indeed became the center of world maritime trade, as evidenced by Jacob's description of the scene when he first arrived in Zayton Port, "On the day of our arrival, there were at least 15,000 ships on the water. Some of them were from Arabia. Some were from Greater India. Some were from Ceylon. Some were from Java the Less ... Others were from our country or other kingdoms of the Franks." Quanzhou engaged in trade with many countries and regions, presenting a prosperous scene of "merchants from all nations thronging to Quanzhou amidst the sound of rising tides." However, behind this prosperity lay untold hardships.

On an island in Indonesia called Wenlaogu (today's Maluku), the local people eagerly awaited the arrival of Chinese merchant ships every year. They raised a special breed of chicken called Wumei Chicken. People there regarded the birth of this type of chicken as an omen of the arrival of Tang ships: whenever the first chick hatched from its eggshell, a Tang ship would definitely arrive, and when the second hatched, a second Tang ship would certainly appear. The simple story reminds us of the arduous journey these ships undertook to reach distant lands, and it also shows the local people's eager expectation of building trade relations with the Chinese merchants.

宋代，出海经商的人必须遵从各地不同的贸易习俗。在渤泥国，即加里曼丹岛北部文莱一带的古国，商船到达后，这里的统治者会携带眷属及随从登船慰问，中国商人会用华丽的锦铺设船板，恭敬迎接，用甜美的酒款待他们，再把金银器皿等各种礼物按不同等级赠送给他们。泊船登岸后，也还不会马上谈论买卖交易的事。来渤泥的商人会带一两个擅长做饭的厨师一同前往，他们每天都会把中国美食敬献给这里的统治者。如此往来几个月，才请统治者及其左右随从商定货品价格。价格确定之后，便鸣鼓召唤远近的人们自由开展贸易。如果价格尚未确定就私自贸易，是要受罚的。船返航的时候，统治者会摆宴斟酒宴请商人，并视其心意赠予一些番布等礼品。

During the Song Dynasty, people engaged in overseas trade had to abide by various local trading customs. In the ancient Kingdom of Borneo, located in the northern part of Kalimantan Island, around the present-day area of Brunei, when Chinese merchant ships arrived, the local ruler would board the ships with his family and attendants to offer greetings. The Chinese traders would use gorgeous brocade to carpet the deck and respectfully welcome them, treating them with sweet wine. They would also present various gifts, including gold and silver utensils, and other items of different grades, to them. Upon anchoring the ships, discussions about trade and business would not be initiated immediately. The visiting merchants would bring along one or two skilled cooks to prepare Chinese cuisine daily as offerings to the local ruler. This exchange of hospitality would continue for several months before the traders could negotiate prices for their goods with the ruler and their attendants. Once the prices were agreed upon, the traders would beat drums to call people from near and far to freely engage in trade. Engaging in unauthorized trade before the prices were set would result in punishment. When the ships were about to return, the ruler would hold a banquet, serve wine, and invite the merchants to join. Based on the ruler's appreciation, the merchants might be presented with some local fabrics and other goods as gifts before their departure.

在文莱发现的逝于渤泥的泉州判院“蒲公”之墓，南宋景定五年（1264）立。（成冬冬 摄）
Tomb of Mr. Pu, built in 1264 and discovered in Brunei, in memory of an official of Quanzhou who died in Borneo. (Photo by Cheng Dongdong)

商人抵达三屿后，每遇一处聚落，并不敢停船登岸，而是先把船停在中流的地方，敲鼓以吸引聚落居民的注意。当地的商人们争先驾驶小船而来。中国客商带来了瓷器、白锡、有花纹的绢、五色烧珠等商品，当地商人则带来优良的吉贝、黄蜡、番布、椰心席子等。经过一番讨价还价，如果价格谈不拢，便需要有声望的商业首领亲自去讨论，留下一两个人作为人质，然后登岸交易，待交易完毕，便归还人质。中国商船在这处聚落停泊约三四天，便掉转船头，去其他地方继续开展贸易活动。

宋元时期也有许多福建商人到占城进行贸易，泉州商人更是受到热烈欢迎。商人到达占城后，有时会有当地妇女登上船，与商人配成佳偶。贸易工作完成后，只好以泪相别，待到第二年船来时，他们才能再续前缘。

繁荣的海外贸易，对商人不仅意味着财富，也可能意味着走上一条不归路。汪大渊在《岛夷志略》中提到，泉州吴宅派遣百余人到古里地闷（今帝汶岛）开展贸易活动，竟然“死者十八九，间存一二，而多羸弱乏力，驾舟随风回舶。”海外贸易虽然要面对很多凶险，但它所带来的巨额利润却使人趋之若鹜。至今横卧海底、满载陶瓷等货物的沉船，仍在哀悼着海外贸易路上的逝者。

In the Three Isles, when merchants arrived at each local community, they dared not anchor their ships and disembark immediately. Instead, they would stop their boats in the middle of the midstream and beat drums to attract people from the local community. The local merchants would vie to row their small boats to approach the visiting merchants. Chinese traders brought various goods such as porcelain, tin, patterned silk, and glass beads, while the local merchants offered excellent ceiba, beeswax, cloth, and mats woven from coconut fibre, among other items. After some bargaining, if the prices could not be agreed upon, a venerable business chief would negotiate in person, leaving one or two members behind as hostages. Then they went ashore to trade. Once the trade was completed, the hostages would be returned. After anchoring in the region for about three to four days, Chinese merchant ships would turn their bows to other places to continue their trading activities.

During the Song and Yuan dynasties, many Fujian merchants went to Champa for trade, and Quanzhou merchants, in particular, were warmly welcomed. Sometimes, when merchants arrived in Champa, they were greeted by local women who would board their ships and become their wives. When the merchants completed their trades, these women bid them farewell with tears, and they could only reunite when the ships returned the following year, continuing their bonds.

The prosperity of overseas trade offered not only wealth to these merchants but also potential risks. According to the records in *A Brief Account of Island Inhabitants* by Wang Dayuan, Wu's family in Quanzhou sent over a hundred people to Gulidimen (present-day Timor Island) for trade, but unfortunately, "eighty or ninety percent of them died. Those who survived were weak with little strength, eventually returning to Quanzhou with the wind." Despite the dangers involved in overseas trade, the enormous profits it brought attracted merchants scrambling to participate in. Even today, shipwrecks lying horizontally on the seabed, filled with cargoes like ceramics, continue to mourn for those who died on the path of overseas trade.

丰硕的进出口货物

宋元泉州“船货充羡”，“有蕃舶之饶，杂货山积”，东西方之间来往的贸易品很多。进口货物以香料药物为大宗，进口的品种多、数量大、用途广。据《宋会要辑稿》记载，北宋建隆元年（960）至南宋淳熙五年（1178）的两百多年间，外国使节进贡礼品共计 633 次，其中明确有香料药物的占 98 次之多。北宋太平兴国七年（982），宋朝廷记录的香料药物有降真香、檀香、丁香、龙脑、胡椒等共计 37 种，至南宋绍兴三年（1133）增至 200 多种，南宋绍兴十一年（1141）超过了 300 种。

在 1974 年出土的泉州湾宋代海船的船舱里，发掘出 4,700 多斤未脱水的香料，为宋元繁荣的“香料之路”提供了实物证明。香料在宋元时期人们的日常生活中扮演着重要角色。据传，北宋名臣赵抃酷爱焚香，他居住的地方，人离开数月香气不散；每次解衣则置于大焙上，焙下薰炉香薰不绝。宋元时期的泉州人，无论贫富，在岁除新年之际，都会燃烧降真香“如燔柴”。泉州人还会用香木雕刻佛像。元末明初的一位僧人曾在诗中描绘泉州“满城香气栴檀绕”。

除了香料药物，宋元泉州从海外进口的物品还有宝物珍玩、原材料、纺织品、金属器物、日杂百货、副食品等，包括槟榔、蔷薇水、珍珠、宝石、花布、白银、琉璃瓶、藤席、酒、万年枣等百余种。

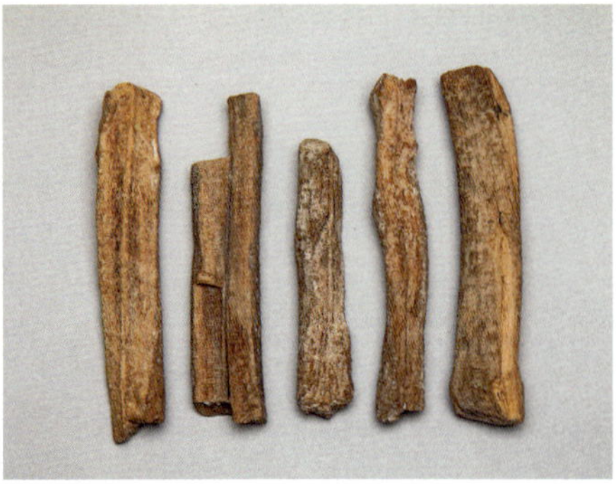

泉州湾宋代海船出水的香料木。（成冬冬 摄）
Aromatic wood discovered in the Song Dynasty Oceangoing Ship at Quanzhou Bay. (Photo by Cheng Dongdong)

泉州湾宋代海船出水的安息香。（成冬冬 摄）
Benzoin discovered in the Song Dynasty Oceangoing Ship at Quanzhou Bay. (Photo by Cheng Dongdong)

Abundant Imports and Exports

During the Song-Yuan period, Quanzhou was known for "its abundant commodities for maritime trade", "and there were lots of foreign ships with goods piled high." Trade between the East and the West involved a wide range of commodities. Spices and medicinal herbs were the major imported goods, with a huge selection of varieties and in large quantities. They were widely used in everyday life. According to *Collected Statutes of the Song Dynasty*, in the span of over 200 years from 960 to 1178, there were a total of 633 instances of foreign envoys presenting tribute gifts, 98 of which specifically mentioned spices and medicinal herbs. In 982, the Song court recorded 37 medicinal substances, including items such as rosewood heart wood, sandalwood, cloves, borneol, and pepper. By 1133, the number of the types of medicinal substances had increased to over 200, and by 1141, it had surpassed 300.

In the Song Dynasty Oceangoing Ship at Quanzhou Bay unearthed in 1974, more than 4,700 *jin* (a Chinese unit of weight) of undried spices were discovered, providing tangible evidence for the flourishing "Spice Route" of the Song-Yuan period. Spices played a significant role in the daily life of people during this era. It is said that Zhao Bian, a renowned official of the Northern Song Dynasty, had a strong affinity for burning incense. The place where he resided remained fragrant for months even when he was away, and whenever he undressed, he would place his clothes on a large censer, from which the fragrance of the burning incense kept emanating. For the people of Quanzhou during this era, regardless of their wealth, burning rosewood heart wood "like burning firewood" was a traditional Chinese New Year festivity. Additionally, they were skilled in using aromatic wood to carve Buddhist statues. A monk living in the late Yuan Dynasty and the early Ming Dynasty once described Quanzhou in his poem as a city "filled with the fragrance of sandalwood."

Apart from spices and medicinal herbs, the goods imported from abroad during the Song-Yuan period included precious items, raw materials, textiles, metalware, daily necessities, and non-staple food. These goods encompassed a wide range of items, such as betel nuts, rosewater, pearls, gemstones, floral fabrics, silver, glass bottles, woven mats, wine, and dried dates, totaling over a hundred varieties.

宋元出口货物以瓷器为大宗。目前泉州已发现的宋元时期窑址 70 余处，分布在泉州的德化、永春、安溪、南安、晋江、泉港等地，在宋元时曾向世界源源不断地输送瓷器。其中，磁灶窑、德化窑两大窑系的产业规模、产品种类和数量都各领风骚，均在宋元时期达到其窑业生产的顶峰。

宋元时期的海上丝绸之路东至高丽、日本，南达东南亚诸国和印度，西至波斯湾和东非各港口。出口海外的陶瓷器，是重要的贸易品，因此，海上丝绸之路也被称为“陶瓷之路”。它们在装船时基本是“大小相套，无少隙地”。

Porcelain was the most prominent export commodity in the Song and Yuan dynasties. Currently, over 70 kiln sites dating back to the Song-Yuan period have been discovered in Quanzhou, scattering in regions such as Dehua, Yongchun, Anxi, Nan'an, Jinjiang, and Quangang. These sites continuously supplied the world with ceramics during that period. Among them, Cizao Kilns and Dehua Kilns distinguished themselves as large production centers in terms of scale, variety, and quantity of products, reaching their peak in the Song and Yuan dynasties.

The Maritime Silk Road during the Song-Yuan period extended eastward to Goryeo and Japan, southward to Southeast Asian countries and India, and westward to the Persian Gulf and ports in East Africa. These routes were also known as the "Ceramic Road," as ceramics for export were important commodities on the Road. When loaded onto ships, "the ceramics were carefully arranged to maximize space, with smaller ones put into bigger ones, making sure there were no gaps between the items."

从目前已经出土的“华光礁Ⅰ号”“南海Ⅰ号”“新安沉船”等宋元时期的沉船，都发掘出了大量外销陶瓷器。在菲律宾、文莱、马来西亚、泰国、印度甚至遥远的非洲东海岸的埃及、坦桑尼亚，都出土了大量中国陶瓷器，其数量之巨大，令人惊叹。

从泉州出口的贸易品除陶瓷器外，还有纺织品、金属制品、杂货、药材等，包括白丝、舟山锦、龙缎、金器、铜鼎、铜盘、铁块、漆器、桐油、伞、琴、阮、糖霜、川芎、白芷、硫黄等。

Shipwrecks from the Song-Yuan period, such as the "Huaguangjiao No. 1," "Nanhai No. 1," and "Xin'an," have been excavated, revealing a vast number of exported Chinese ceramics. Today, stunningly, large quantities of Chinese ceramics have been unearthed in countries like the Philippines, Brunei, Malaysia, Thailand, India, and even as far as the east coast of Africa, including Egypt and Tanzania.

In addition to ceramics, other trade goods exported from Quanzhou included textiles, metal products, groceries, and medicinal herbs. These items encompassed a wide range, such as white silk, Zhoushan brocade, Longduan silk, goldware, bronze cauldrons, bronze trays, iron blocks, lacquerware, tung oil, umbrellas, musical instruments like *qin* and *ruan*, sugar icing, Sichuan lovage rhizome, angelica, sulfur, and more.

德化窑址。（陈英杰 摄）
Sites of Dehua Kilns. (Photo by Chen Yingjie)

全社会参与的海洋贸易

海外贸易带来的巨大财富，不仅吸引了朝廷、贵族们的注意，越来越多的商人也开始在这一领域谋求出路。海外贸易虽然能带来丰厚的利润，但是风险无处不在。据《萍洲可谈》记载，由于海盗出没，商人们就选择拧在一起干，提高远洋贸易的安全性。他们在船舱里各得数尺地方，专门存放自己的货物，到了晚上，人就睡在货上。为实现利润最大化，货品摆得都很紧凑，大、小型的陶瓷器会套在一起装货，几乎不留一点剩余空间。

对于无力自备海船的小商人来说，充当有船的大商人的“人伴”是另一种参与海外贸易的办法。大家“结为一甲，互相作保”，在海上成为各司其职的水手或“搭客”，顺便也捎带货物做买卖。据《宋会要辑稿》记载，宋代的五百料船，多是留八分装货，留二分允许船上人员装载私人货物。这个办法沿用至近代，船主不付薪水，而是预留一百担的吨位给船员。例如，火长有工资，另外还可以自带货物五十担，其他人员没有工资，但是可以携带一定比例的货物，舵工二十五担，碇工九担，水手七担，这种经营模式称为“以舱代薪”。

泉州海外交通史博物馆福船横剖面隔舱及货物场景再现，货物装船实现了船舱空间的充分利用。（段燕飞 摄）
A scene replication in Quanzhou Maritime Museum: the cross-section of the *Fu-Chuan* compartments and cargo placement to showcase the efficient utilization of cargo holds during loading. (Photo by Duan Yanfei)

Ocean Trade Involving the Entire Society

Overseas trade brought immense wealth, which not only attracted the attention of the court and nobles but also inspired more and more merchants to earn their livelihood from overseas trade. While overseas trade could yield substantial profits, it was fraught with risks. In *Pingzhou Table Talk*, it is documented that due to the presence of pirates, traders chose to huddle together and work as a group, to improve the safety of long-distance overseas trade activities. They would secure an area of a few square feet in the hold, where they would store their goods. At night, they would sleep on top of their merchandise. To maximize profits, the cargo was packed tightly together, nesting differently sized ceramic wares to utilize every bit of available space.

For small merchants who couldn't afford their own ships, becoming companions to wealthy merchants was another way to participate in overseas trade. They would "form a group and cross guarantee," and become sailors or "companions" on the sea, fulfilling their respective functions, while also engaging in buying and selling goods on the side. According to *Collected Statutes of the Song Dynasty*, ships with a capacity of 500 *liao* (a Chinese unit of timber volume) often reserved four fifths of space for cargo and allowed the ship's crew to use the remaining part for their personal goods. This practice continued even in the early modern era. Instead of paying wages to the crew, ship owners would reserve a certain tonnage capable of carrying 100 *dan* (a Chinese unit of weight) of goods for crew members. For example, *huo zhang*, the navigator, could earn a wage, and could also bring 50 *dan* of personal goods. Other crew members did not receive wages, but they could carry a certain proportion of goods. For instance, the helmsman could carry 25 *dan*, the anchor worker 9, the sailors 7, and so on. This business model was known as "pay with cargo space."

从一些已出土的文物中，我们能更直观地看出这种结伴而行、广泛参与的航海贸易活动。1974 年出土的泉州湾宋代海船上有一批木牌签，挂在各种货物上，木牌签上体现了人名、职位或店名信息。例如，“朱库”可能是一位在船上担任直库一职的朱姓人员，管理武器；“张什”可能是一位处理船上日常杂务的张姓人员；“丘碇”可能是一位丘姓碇工，管理固定船舶的碇；“张绊”可能是一位张姓缆工，管理船上的索缆；“安厨”可能是一位负责做饭的安姓厨工；“礼天”可能是职位名称，负责船上举行的祭祀等仪式；“杨工”“尤工”“三九工”应为船上普通水手。此外，船上还有“南家”货牌，用于标记居住在泉州的宋皇族后裔的货品，以及“曾幹”“林幹”“张幹”货牌，用于标记市舶司内一些官吏的货品，还能见到具体人名如“吴兴”“小陈”“王美”，以及阿拉伯裔人“哑哩”等。这些名称有一部分是船员名字，有一部分很可能与航海背后的资本组成和社会关系有关。

泉州湾宋代海船出土的木牌签。（成冬冬 摄）
Wooden tags unearthed from the Song Dynasty Oceangoing Ship at Quanzhou Bay. (Photo by Cheng Dongdong)

From some unearthed artifacts, we can gain a better visual understanding of the maritime trade activities involving companionship and widespread participation. Among the artifacts found on the Song Dynasty Oceangoing Ship at Quanzhou Bay excavated in 1974, there is a group of wooden tags hanging on various types of cargo. Names, positions, or shop names were written on these wooden tags. For example:

Zhu Ku（朱库）: "Zhu" is a surname, and "Ku" signifies the position of the "Zhi Ku"（直库）, who oversees weapons on the ship.

Zhang Shi（张什）: The person surnamed "Zhang" is responsible for handling daily affairs on the ship.

Qiu Ding（丘碇）: The person surnamed "Qiu" manages the ship's anchor.

Zhang Ban（张绊）: The person surnamed "Zhang" is responsible for the mooring and towing ropes on the ship.

An Chu（安厨）: The person surnamed "An" is responsible for cooking meals on the ship.

Li Tian（礼天）: "Li Tian" is probably a position that involves the responsibility of performing sacrifices and other ceremonies on the ship.

Yang Gong（杨工）, You Gong（尤工）, San Jiu Gong（三九工）: These are likely ordinary sailors or crew members.

In addition, there are cargo tags of "Nan Jia" (literally translated as the family in the south), which mark the goods belonging to the descendants of the Song imperial family residing in Quanzhou. There are also cargo tags bearing the marks "Zeng Gan"（曾幹）, "Lin Gan"（林幹）, and "Zhang Gan"（张幹）, which indicate the Maritime Trade Office officials' ownership of goods. Specific personal names such as "Wu Xing"（吴兴）, "Xiao Chen"（小陈）, "Wang Mei"（王美）, and even Arabic names like "Ali"（哑哩）and others, can also be seen. Some of these names are likely the names of the crew members, while others might be associated with the composition of capital and the social relationships involved in the ship's voyage behind the maritime trade.

在日本也收藏着一件珍贵的文物，它是宋代两浙路市舶司批准泉州舶商李充赴日贸易的公凭。上面详细记录了货品的种类、数量，以及所有船上人员的姓名，另外还有三位保人的姓名。当时出海贸易，要获得批准之后才可以出行，而且需要三位保人作担保，进出口都不许隐瞒货品，否则会受到处罚。该船上人员构成与泉州湾宋代海船也大致类似。中国古人外出航海，与陆地上的人会建立担保关系，它的脉系是庞杂的。可以说，宋元泉州的海上贸易是一项多种势力、多个阶层共同参与的在海外追逐利润的探险活动。

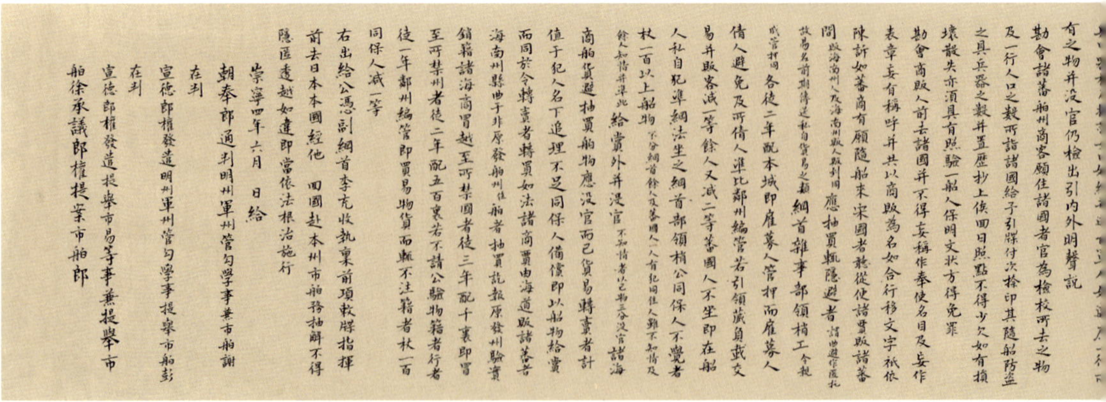
有之物并没官仍檢出引内外明聲說
勘會諸蕃舶州商客願往諸國者官為檢校所去之物
及一行人口之數所詣諸國給予引牒付次捺印其隨船防盗
之具兵器之數并置歷抄上俟回日照點不得少欠如有損
壞散失亦須具有照驗一船人保明文狀方得免罪
勘會商販人前去諸國并不得妄稱作奉使名目及妄作
表章妄有稱呼并共以商販為名如合行移文字祇依
陳訴如蕃商有願隨船來宋國者聽從便諸販諸蕃
間 販海南州人及海南州販人販到回 應抽買輒隱避者 謂曲避作匿私
故易名前期傳送私自貿易之類 綱首雜事部領梢工 令親
戚管押同 各徒二年配本城即雇募人管押而雇募人
倩人避免及所倩人準比鄰州編管若引領藏匿或交
易并販客減一等餘人又減二等蕃國人不坐即在船
人私自犯準綱法坐之綱首部領梢公同保人不覺者
杖一百以上船物 不分綱首餘人及蕃國人一人有犯同住人雖不知情及
餘人知情并準此 給賞外并沒官 不知情者以己物三分沒官 諸海
商船貨避抽買船物應沒官而已貨易轉賣者計
值于犯人名下追理不足同保人備償即以船物給賞
而同於令轉賣者轉買如法諸商賈由海道販諸蕃者
海南州縣曲于非原發舶州住舶者抽買訖報原發州驗實
銷籍諸海商冒越至所禁國者徒三年配千裏即冒
至所禁州者徒二年配五百裏若不請公驗物籍者行者
徒一年鄰州編管即買易物貨而輒不注籍者杖一百
同保人減一等
右出給公憑副綱首李充收執稟前項敕牒指揮
前去日本國經他　回國赴本州市舶務抽解不得
隱匿透越如違即當依法根治施行
崇寧四年六月　日給
朝奉郎通判明州軍州管勾學事兼市舶謝
在判
宣德郎權發遣明州軍州管勾學事提舉市舶彭
在判
宣德郎權發遣提舉市易等事兼提舉市
舶徐承議郎權提案市舶郎

李充赴日贸易的公凭（复制件）。（泉州海外交通史博物馆 供图）
Duplicate of the official document approving Li Chong's trade trip to Japan. (Courtesy of Quanzhou Maritime Museum)

There is a precious historical relic in Japan: an official document issued by the Maritime Trade Office of Liangzhe Lu, approving a trade trip to Japan led by a Quanzhou merchant named Li Chong. The document contains detailed information about the types and quantities of goods, the names of all crew members on board, and the names of three guarantors. During that time, maritime trade required official approval and the support of three guarantors. Importers and exporters were prohibited from concealing any goods; otherwise, they would face punishment. The composition of the people on board is somewhat similar to that of Song Dynasty Oceangoing Ship at Quanzhou Bay. Ancient Chinese people going on seafaring journeys built guarantee relationships with people on land. The system was complex. It can be said that the maritime trade of Quanzhou in Song and Yuan dynasties was an adventurous pursuit of profits overseas involving multiple forces and social classes working together.

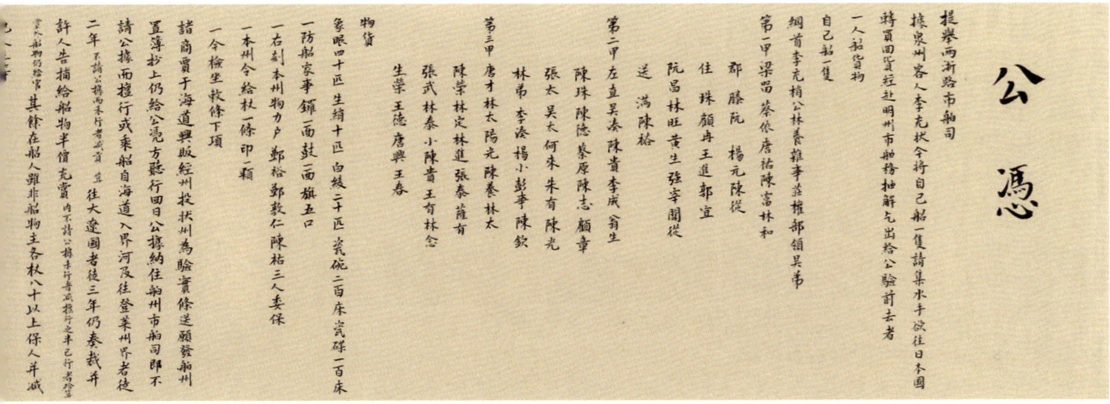
公憑
提舉兩浙路市舶司
據泉州客人李充狀今將自己船一隻請集水手欲往日本國
轉買回貨經赴明州市舶務抽解乞出給公驗前去者
一人船貨物
自己船一隻
綱首李充 梢公林養 雜事莊權 部領吳弟
第一甲 梁富 蔡依 唐祐 陳富 林和
郡 滕 阮 楊元 陳從
住 珠 顧冉 王進 郭宜
阮昌 林旺 黃生 強宰 關從
送 满 陳裕
第二甲 左直 吳湊 陳貴 李成 翁生
陳珠 陳德 蔡原 陳志 顧章
張太 吳太 何來 朱有 陳光
林弟 李湊 楊小 彭事 陳欽
第三甲 唐才 林太 陽光 陳養 林太
陳榮 林定 林進 張泰 薩有
張武 林泰 小陳 貴 王有 林念
生榮 王德 唐興 王春
物貨
象眼四十疋 生絹十疋 白綾二十疋 瓷碗二百床 瓷碟一百床
一防船家事 鑼一面 鼓一面 旗五口
一石刻本州物力戶 鄭裕 鄭敦仁 陳祐 三人委保
一本州令給杖一條 印一顆
一今檢坐敕條下項
諸商賈于海道興販經州投狀州為驗實條送願發船州
置簿抄上仍給公憑方聽行回日公據納住船州市舶司即不
請公據而擅行或乘船自海道入界河及往登萊州界者徒
二年 不請公據而未行者減二等 往大遼國者徒三年仍奏裁并
許人告捕給船物半價充賞 內不請公據未行者減擬行之半已行者給當
賞人船物仍給官 其餘在船人雖非船物主各杖八十以上保人并減

外国人眼中宋元泉州的繁盛之景

The Prosperity of Song-Yuan Quanzhou in the Eyes of Foreigners

不远万里来泉贸易

Traveling More than Ten Thousand *Li* to Do Trade in Quanzhou

国际巨港：比任何一个港口的船都多

A Giant International Port: Docking Ships Are More than Anywhere Else

吸引外国人聚集的大都市

A Metropolitan City Attracting Foreigners

光明之城的大市场

An Enormous Market in the City of Light

一千人的作坊与行会组织

Thousand-People Workshops and Guilds

富商之家

Wealthy Merchants

东门百戏

A Hundred Theatrical Troupes by the East Gate

发达的出版行业

The Well-Developed Publishing Businesses

热衷采购中国货

A Passion for Goods Made in China

宋元时期，曾到访泉州的旅行家一定不少，但留下文字记载者寥寥无几。雅各于南宋末年来到泉州经商，写下《光明之城》一书，详细记载了泉州当时的社会状况，这本书直到1997年才面世。曾在元朝供职的意大利旅行家、商人马可·波罗足迹遍布中国，从泉州返回家乡后，作家鲁思梯谦将他口述的见闻整理成《马可·波罗行纪》。摩洛哥学者、旅行家伊本·白图泰以印度使节的身份于元至正六年（1346）来到泉州，游历了不少城市，他将自己的旅行记录下来，写成《伊本·白图泰游记》。在他们的笔墨中，既有繁盛壮观的宋元海洋商贸盛况，也有细腻动人的日常生活场景。

1999 年 2 月在泉州举办的“《光明之城》手稿的发现及其研究”座谈会。（成冬冬 摄）
Academic Workshop on *The City of Light* held in Quanzhou in February 1999. (Photo by Cheng Dongdong)

During the Song and Yuan dynasties, there were undoubtedly many travelers who had been to Quanzhou, but only a few of them left written records. Jacob arrived in Quanzhou for business during the late Southern Song Dynasty. He wrote a book called *The City of Light*, which provided detailed accounts of the social conditions in Quanzhou at that time. However, this book did not come to light until 1997. Italian traveler and merchant Marco Polo, who served in various capacities in Yuan government, had extensively traveled through China. After he departed from Quanzhou and returned to his homeland, Marco Polo told his tales of travel to Rustichello, an Italian writer, who wrote the book known as *The Travels of Marco Polo*. Ibn Battuta, a Moroccan scholar and traveler, visited Quanzhou in 1346 in the role of an envoy from India. He traveled to many cities and chronicled his travel experiences in a work called *Travels*. In the writings of these travelers, we can find descriptions of the flourishing and magnificent maritime trade during the Song and Yuan dynasties, as well as detailed accounts of moving scenes of daily life.

不远万里来泉贸易

雅各一路航海的最终目的地正是泉州。有的学者甚至认为，宋元时期一些意大利港口城市的兴盛，得益于与中国开展了贸易。雅各对泉州人喜爱的贸易品极为熟悉。从欧洲出发时，他“带了许多货物，有天鹅绒布匹和羊毛，也有我们的金线，在中国，人们会为它付大价钱”。在法马古斯塔，他购买了许多优质细棉布被子，因为他认为中国人在冬天非常需要它们。在考姆萨，他购买了很多优质香料，他认为印度和中国的偶像崇拜者愿意购买这些香料，尤其是达法罗的乳香。在齐希，他发现了许多质量很好的麝香，他提到，中国人会用四倍于它重量的银子来购买。在芒吉阿勒，他采购了种类繁多的胡椒，有黑色的，也有白色的，他说：“胡椒在中国和在我们国家一样昂贵。”芒吉阿勒也有檀木、芦荟，以及其他的香树，这里的樟脑质量也很好，它们“在中国与黄金一样贵重”。

泉州湾宋代海船出水的胡椒子。（成冬冬 摄）
The pepper seeds salvaged from the Song Dynasty Oceangoing Ship at Quanzhou Bay. (Photo by Cheng Dongdong)

Traveling More than Ten Thousand Li *to Do Trade in Quanzhou*

Jacob set his destination in Quanzhou on his maritime journey. Some scholars even argue that the prosperity of certain Italian port cities during the Song and Yuan dynasties was due to their trade with China. Jacob was familiar with the trade goods highly sought after in Quanzhou. When he departed from Europe, he brought lots of goods with him, like velvet cloth, wool and gold thread produced in Italy, which he believed people in China would be glad to buy at great expense. In Famagusta, he bought many high-quality quilts made of fine cotton cloth, for he thought they were very much needed by Chinese people in winter. In Cormosa, he purchased many high-quality spices. He noted that idol worshippers in India and China were very willing to buy these spices, especially the Dafaro frankincense. In Chisi, he found a large quantity of excellent musk and mentioned that the Chinese would buy them with silver ingots four times the weight of the goods. In Mangialur, Jacob continued to purchase various kinds of pepper, like black pepper and white pepper. He remarked that pepper in China was as expensive as it was in his country. There were also sandalwood, aloe, and other fragrant wood in Mangialur, and its camphor was of good quality. They were as valuable as gold in China.

之后，他又大量采购了优质的丁香、豆蔻和珊瑚。他说：“这些商品对中国人来说是珍贵的，因为他们要用来绕在他们的妇女和他们偶像的脖子上。”他从巴鲁奇·埃布里奥那里获取了一些购物上的指导，得知“味道甜美的树，特别是檀木和芦荟，中国的贵族以及有钱的商人都非常看重，他们在房屋的支柱以及大门上都使用这些东西。贩运这些东西，可以从他们那儿得到很大的收益”。他采购了一大批香树、香水以及雕刻得很精巧的象牙梳子，因为他听说中国的贵族妇女常使用香水，把香水放在丝袋里系在腰间，发间也会插象牙梳子。

他带着满载货物的船来到泉州，以极高的价格将船上的胡椒、芦荟木、檀香木、樟脑、香水、珠宝、衣料等卖给城中的商人。他不无得意地写道，有人说在中国的土地上从来没有哪个同乡能像他一样赚取如此丰厚的利润。

Subsequently, Jacob bought a large quantity of cloves, cardamom, and coral. He mentioned that the goods were precious to Chinese because they liked to wear them around the necks of women and idols. Jacob received guidance on purchasing from Baruch Ebreo and learned that the nobility and wealthy merchants in China attached great importance to sweet smelling woods, sandalwood and aloe in particular, and that they used these goods on pillars of their houses and the gates. Transporting these goods for sale could, therefore, generate huge profits. He also purchased lots of fragrant woods, perfumes and intricately carved ivory combs because he heard that Chinese noble women commonly used perfumes and carried them in silk bags tied around their waists, while ivory combs were adorned on their heads.

Arriving in Quanzhou with his cargo-laden ships, he sold pepper, aloe wood, sandalwood, camphor, perfumes, jewelry, fabrics and more to the local merchants at extremely high prices. Jacob proudly noted that someone said that no other compatriot could earn such abundant profits as he did in China.

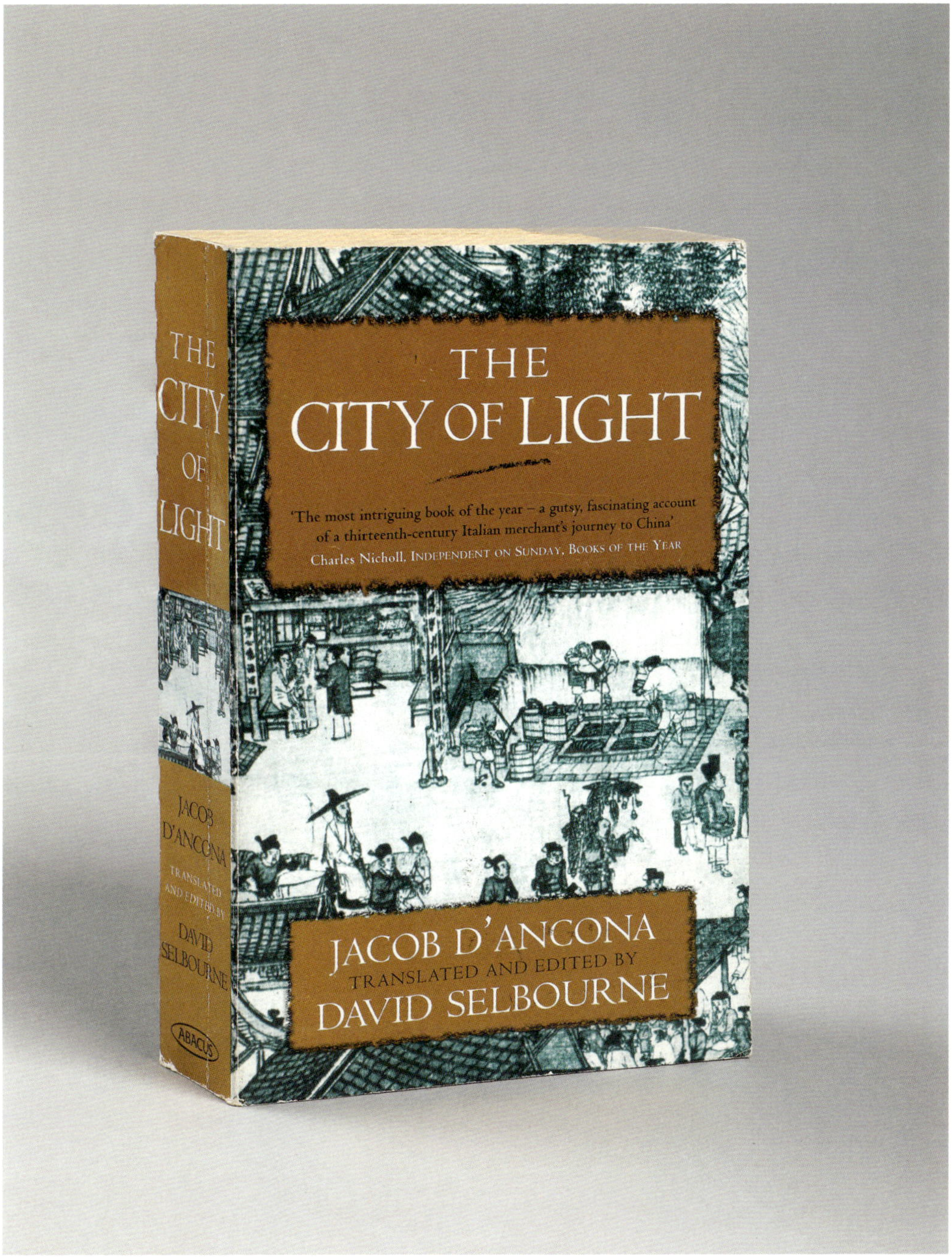

《光明之城》。（成冬冬 摄）
The City of Light. (Photo by Cheng Dongdong)

国际巨港：比任何一个港口的船都多

马可·波罗写道："此城为世界最大良港之一，商人商货聚积之多，几难信有其事。""由是商货宝石珍珠输入之多竟至不可思议……我敢言亚历山大或他港运载胡椒一船赴诸基督教国，乃至此刺桐港者，则有船舶百余，所以大汗在此港征收税课，为额极巨。"

伊本·白图泰则这样描述泉州："这是一巨大城市，此地织造的锦缎和绸缎，也以刺桐命名。该城的港口是世界大港之一，甚至是最大的港口。我看到港内停有大艟克约百艘，小船多得无数。这个港口是一个伸入陆地的巨大港湾，以至与大江汇合。该城花园很多，房舍位于花园中央……"

A Giant International Port: Docking Ships Are More than Anywhere Else

Marco Polo wrote about Quanzhou: "This city is one of the world's largest and finest harbors, and the number of merchants and goods gathered here is so vast that it is almost unbelievable." He further noted, "An incredible number of gemstones and pearls are imported to Zayton from all over the world ... I would say if one ship loaded with pepper sails from the port of Alexandria or other ports to the Christian countries, there will be more than a hundred ships carrying pepper to Zayton Port. The amount of taxes collected by the Great Khan in Zayton was astonishingly high."

Ibn Battuta described Quanzhou as follows: "This is a huge city known for its production of brocades and silks, named after Zayton. The port of this city is one of the world's great ports, possibly even the largest. I saw around a hundred large ships and countless small boats dock in the harbor. This port is a vast bay extending into the land, and it converges with a large river. The city has many gardens, and houses are situated in the midst of these gardens."

伫立在泉州海外交通史博物馆的伊本·白图泰塑像。（陈起拓 摄）
The statue of Ibn Battuta standing in Quanzhou Maritime Museum. (Photo by Chen Qituo)

雅各的描写更为细致：泉州被高山环绕成为一个躲避风暴的港口。这里的江水广大宽阔，奔流不息。每年都有几千艘载着胡椒的船停泊卸货。“我看见停泊在这儿的大海船、三桅帆船和小型商船比我以前在任何一个港口看到的都要多，甚至超过了威尼斯。而且，中国的商船也是人们能够想象出的最大的船只，有的有 6 层桅杆，4 层甲板，12 张大帆，可以装载 1,000 多人。”

泉州湾古船陈列馆内悬挂的《涨海声中万国商》大型国画作品。（成冬冬 摄）

Merchants from All Nations Thronging to Quanzhou Amidst the Sound of Rising Tides, a huge Chinese painting hung in the Exhibition Hall of Ancient Ship in Quanzhou Bay. (Photo by Cheng Dongdong)

Jacob's description of Quanzhou is even more detailed: Quanzhou is surrounded by high mountains, making it a port providing shelter from storms. The river here is vast and wide, flowing endlessly. Every year, thousands of ships carrying pepper anchored here and unloaded their cargo. He said, "I saw more large seagoing ships, three-masted vessels, and small merchant ships docked here than I had seen in any other port before, even surpassing Venice. Moreover, Chinese merchant ships are the largest one can imagine, some with six masts, four decks, and twelve large sails, capable of accommodating over 1,000 people."

吸引外国人聚集的大都市

宋元时期的泉州人一定比今天的泉州人见到的外国人还多。雅各曾说刺桐城仿佛不是中国人的城市，而是“整个世界的一座城市”。这些外国人分别居住在不同的区域，阿拉伯人、法兰克人、亚美尼亚人、犹太人、日耳曼人、意大利人等都有自己的居住区，甚至每个区域内又细分不同的聚居地。

在刺桐城中可以听到上百种不同的口音。刺桐城内包容了各种民族、各种教派，所有人都获得允许按照自己的信仰行事，许多民族、教派还有自己的教堂、医院、学堂和墓地。中国人自古以来秉承的开放包容的理念，造就了刺桐城多元文化的相融共通，他们不强迫任何人违背自己的志愿住在中国，也不会将任何一个愿意与中国人相处的外国人拒之门外。

在开放多元的泉州，基督教堂与开元寺东西塔静静对望。（傅捷雄 摄）
In the open and inclusive city of Quanzhou, the Christian Church standing silently facing the East and West Pagodas of Kaiyuan Temple. (Photo by Fu Jiexiong)

A Metropolitan City Attracting Foreigners

The people of Quanzhou in the Song and Yuan dynasties must have met a greater number of foreigners than present-day Quanzhou residents. Jacob once described Quanzhou as a city that did not seem to belong to the Chinese but to the entire world. Foreigners lived in different areas of the city. Arabs, Franks, Armenians, Jews, Germans, Italians, and others, each had their own residential neighborhood, and each neighborhood was even further subdivided into distinct settlement areas.

Within the city, one could hear a hundred different accents. Zayton city embraced diverse ethnic groups and various religious groups, allowing everyone to practice their beliefs freely. Many ethnic groups and religious groups had their own churches, hospitals, schools, and cemeteries. The intercultural integration and communication in Zayton city resulted from Chinese people's value of being open and inclusive that had taken shape since ancient times. They don't force anyone to live against their own will in China, and nor do they exclude any foreigner who is willing to get along with Chinese people.

光明之城的大市场

据雅各介绍，在刺桐城中，“街上有如此众多的油灯和火把，到了晚上，这个城市被映照得特别灿烂，在很远的地方都能看得到它”。因此，人们把这座城市称作光明之城。

数不清的人白天黑夜都挤在市场里，关注着来自各个国家的贵重货物。港口和街道上，几乎挤满了人和运货马车，人们都在为自己的生意忙碌奔波。热闹非凡的市场、庞杂的货物，这样的景象世间少有。雅各甚至担心是否有足够的食物来养活这么多人。

据雅各的观察，刺桐城有着世界上最多的商店，商店里香料、丝绸、珠宝、酒、油膏、颜料等商品应有尽有。在这里能买到各种各样的药品，如治感冒的药、驱赶昆虫的药膏、消肿止痛的草药。卖丝绸的商店汇集成一条街，销售的丝绸竟不下二百种。有一条街专门卖金银器，集中着萨拉森人和犹太人。此外，还有一条街聚集着药剂师，另一条街上占星家扎堆……人来人往，热闹无比。

刺桐城的每个城门口都有市场，有的门口是丝绸市场，有的门口是香料市场，有的门口是牛市和车市，有的门口是马市，有的门口是乡下人卖谷物的市场，有的门口是大米市场，有的门口是公绵羊和山羊市场，有的门口是海鱼与河鱼市场。此外，还有水果市场、鲜花市场、布匹市场、书籍市场、陶瓷市场、珠宝市场等。这里商品的丰富程度已超越了世人的想象。雅各总结道：“光明之城一带是贸易发达、制造业繁荣的地方，也是买卖兴隆的地区，在这里，商人可以获得高额的利润。”

An Enormous Market in the City of Light

According to Jacob's description, in Zayton city, there were so many oil lamps and torches in the street that the city was illuminated brightly everywhere at night, and could, therefore, be seen from quite far away. As such, the city was nicknamed "the City of Light."

Throughout the day and night, countless people crowded into the market, attentively watching precious goods arriving from various countries. The harbor and streets were packed with people and cargo carts, and people were busy with their businesses. The vibrant market and masses of goods were unparalleled in the world. Jacob even worried if there would be enough food to feed such a great number of people.

Jacob observed that Quanzhou had the largest number of shops in the world, offering a wide variety of goods such as spices, silk, jewelry, wine, ointments, and colors. A diverse range of medicines could be found here, including remedies for colds, insect repellents, and herbal medicines for swelling and pain relief. One street was dedicated to selling silk, offering no less than two hundred varieties. Another street dealt in gold and silver, where Saracens and Jews gathered. Besides, there was a street like a meeting place of pharmacists, and another, of astrologers, and so much more, creating a bustling and lively atmosphere.

At each city gate of Zayton, there was a market: one gate for silk, another for spices, others for cattle and carts, horses, grains sold by countrymen, rice, rams and goats, sea fish and river fish. Besides, there were markets for fruits, flowers, fabrics, books, ceramics, jewelry, and the list went on. The abundance of goods in Quanzhou was beyond imagination. Jacob remarked that "the City of Light" was a place of prosperous trade and thriving manufacturing industry, where merchants had extensive business dealings and gained substantial profits.

一千人的作坊与行会组织

从雅各的描述中，可以判断泉州也是当时中国重要的生产制造基地。这里有许多巨大的作坊，数以百计的男女在一起工作，有的作坊甚至有1,000人之多。这些作坊有的生产金属制品，有的制造瓷花瓶，有的生产丝绸，有的制造纸张……

在这里，城市和农村的边界已经模糊，因为雅各看到城市的居住区几乎与周围的村镇连为一体了。周边一些农村几乎家家都从事制造，家家都成了小作坊，产品运到刺桐城出售。有的生意人会直接到乡下收购货物，比城里便宜很多。

商品经济的发展还促进了刺桐城行会组织的产生和成熟。据雅各介绍，刺桐城内各个行业都有行会组织，为行业从业者提供指导和帮助。泉州当地一些经商的贵族在海外还有自己的代理商。

金交椅山窑址作坊遗址。（成冬冬 摄）
A relic workshop site in Jinjiaoyishan Kilns. (Photo by Cheng Dongdong)

Thousand-People Workshops and Guilds

Based on Jacob's description, Quanzhou was also an important manufacturing base in China during that time. The city housed numerous large workshops where hundreds of men and women worked together, and some workshops even accommodated up to a thousand people. These workshops were involved in various manufacturing activities, producing metal products, porcelain vases, silk, paper, and so on.

The boundary between the city and the countryside had become blurred, as Jacob observed that the residential areas of the city almost merged with the surrounding towns and villages. In some of the surrounding rural areas, almost every household engaged in manufacturing, functioning as a small workshop, and their products were then transported to Zayton city for sale. Some merchants would purchase goods directly from the countryside, which was much cheaper than buying in the city.

The development of the commodity economy also facilitated the emergence and maturation of guild organizations in Zayton city. According to Jacob's account, there were guilds representing various industries in Zayton city, providing guidance and assistance for practitioners within their respective trades. Some nobles involved in trade had their own agents in overseas regions.

富商之家

繁盛的泉州城不乏富商，他们人数多、财富多。

雅各这样描述大商人孙英寿家中的环境：“他的居所真是一个豪华的宫殿，有很多的通道，用于宴饮的亭台、花园，连他家中的地板也使用银子镶嵌。”

这位大商人穿着讲究，衣服用上好的丝绸缝制，鞋子用缎子做成，有问题的地方会立刻要求他的裁缝修改。他用餐时，数十个仆人随时恭候。

富商们的房屋富丽堂皇。他们的房间里，有花费巨资采购来的装饰品、字画和家具。他们热衷于购买珍奇物品，比如以高超技艺打造的可以沙沙作响的金制、银制树叶，以及可以站在树上、能发出鸣叫声的金鹊银燕。富裕家庭的妇人们穿的也是绫罗绸缎，头上戴着珍珠头饰，她们会用香水和明矾洗浴，使全身散发着馥郁的芳香。

宋元泉州富商巨贾之家场景再现。（成冬冬 摄）
A scene replication of a wealthy merchant family in Song-Yuan Quanzhou. (Photo by Cheng Dongdong)

Wealthy Merchants

In the thriving city of Quanzhou, there were many wealthy merchants who possessed a great fortune.

Jacob described what the residence of Sun Yingshou, a wealthy merchant, looked like as follows: "His residence resembles a luxurious palace, where there are many passages, pavilions, and gardens, and even floors are inlaid with silver."

The wealthy merchant paid meticulous attention to his attire. His clothes were tailored from the finest silk, and his shoes were made of satin, and his tailors would immediately be summoned to make alterations if anything was not to his liking. There were dozens of attendants ready to attend to every need when he dined.

The residences of wealthy merchants were magnificent. In their rooms, there were costly decorations, calligraphy and paintings, and furniture. They were wild about purchasing curiosities, such as exquisitely crafted gold and silver leaves that rustled when touched, gold magpies and silver swallows that could stand in the tree and chirp. Women in wealthy families also dressed lavishly, wearing exquisite silk fabrics and pearl headdresses. They would bathe with perfumes and alum, enveloping themselves in a delightful fragrance.

东门百戏

雅各提到，在泉州东门附近，一到晚上便聚集了来此娱乐休闲的人们。这里灯火辉煌，至少有一百个剧团在这里各自搭建舞台，进行表演，每个剧团周围都有一大群人，他们在等待演员表演、乐队演奏。在这里，可以听到叫喊声、喇叭声、鼓声、鼓掌声、戏曲旋律、刀剑撞击声、棍棒敲打声等，年轻的人们沉浸其中。

发达的出版行业

雅各认为刺桐城的印刷和出版行业也很发达，可以带来巨大的利润。在这里，花一点小钱就能买到图书，这对于想了解世界的人来说非常方便。当地人准备好小块的木头，在上面或刻文字，或刻图像，然后用一种褐色的墨水，把这些文字或图像印刷在纸上。用这类方法，便能生产制作很多不同的图书，既有先贤圣哲的著作，也有诗人骚客的作品，还有面向普通百姓的故事、寓言，当然也不乏一些俚俗的内容。在刺桐城，书商可以自由地出售图书。

宋元泉州演出场景再现。（段燕飞 摄）
A scene replication of giving performances in Song-Yuan Quanzhou. (Photo by Duan Yanfei)

A Hundred Theatrical Troupes by the East Gate

Jacob observed that near the eastern gate of Quanzhou, as evening approached, people gathered to seek joy and leisure. The area was illuminated by lanterns and firelight. At least a hundred theatrical troupes set up their stages here to perform. Each troupe was surrounded by crowds of people eagerly awaiting the actors' performances and the music of the bands. The scene was filled with shouts, trumpeting, drumming, applause, the melodies of various theatrical performances, the clashing of swords, and the banging of sticks. Young people were deeply immersed.

The Well-Developed Publishing Businesses

Jacob believed that the printing and publishing industry in Quanzhou was highly developed and lucrative, bringing substantial profits. Here in Quanzhou, it was convenient for people interested in exploring the world to obtain books at an affordable price. Quanzhou residents used small pieces of wood on which they carved characters or images. They then used brown ink to print these characters or images onto paper. This method allowed them to produce various types of books, including works by sages and philosophers, poetry by poets, stories and fables that targeted the common people. There were also some contents tailored to appeal to the masses. In Zayton city, booksellers could freely sell books.

热衷采购中国货

瓷器是泉州生产的一种重要的出口贸易品。马可·波罗提到，泉州人制造瓷器，要先取一种土，室外静置三四十年，使之经历风吹日晒、雨水浇淋，成为精纯的土，适于烧制瓷器。先辈们储存瓷土，自己的子孙使用。伊本·白图泰提到，瓷器在中国可能更为价廉，正如陶器在摩洛哥一样，中国制造的瓷器是最好的，运销到印度、摩洛哥等地。

雅各比他们两个更懂商品和贸易。他了解到刺桐城出售的许多商品是在周边的城镇或村庄里生产的，因此，他也会去周边直接采购货物，那里买到的货物会更加便宜。他购买了以刺桐命名的丝织品——刺桐缎，上面缀满了小珍珠，精致华美。单是瓷碗他就购买了600件，在他眼中，它们“精美得就像玻璃的酒壶……全都是世界上最美丽的瓷器”。

他还采购了口感很好的食糖、养护肾脏和胃的红花、调理牙病的油膏、通便的山扁豆。此外，他还发现了靛蓝、明矾、纸张、油漆、草药等。在亚历山大市场卖出可能不到所有货物的五分之一甚至六分之一时，雅各挣得的钱已经超过了他采购商品所花费的钱了。往返泉州的雅各无疑是幸运的，他顺利返航并挣得了巨大的财富。

德化屈斗宫窑址出土的白瓷蔗段洗。（成冬冬 摄）
Sugarcane-shaped white porcelain brush washer unearthed from the site of Qudougong Kiln in Dehua. (Photo by Cheng Dongdong)

A Passion for Goods Made in China

Porcelain was an important export commodity produced in Quanzhou. According to Marco Polo, the people of Quanzhou obtained a specific type of clay and left it exposed to the elements for thirty to forty years until it turned into fine clay, which was suitable for porcelain making. The ancestors of the locals stored this clay, and their descendants could use it. Ibn Battuta mentioned that porcelain was possibly sold at a lower price in China, just like pottery in Morocco, and that the excellent quality of Chinese porcelain made it highly sought after in places like India and Morocco.

Jacob, more knowledgeable than the above two about commodities and trade, learned that many commodities sold in Zayton city were produced in its surrounding towns or villages. He would, therefore, also go to the surrounding areas to make purchases, where goods were sold at lower prices. He bought Zayton Satin, named after Zayton, which was adorned with small pearls and intricately crafted. It looked gorgeous. He purchased 600 porcelain bowls. In his eyes, the bowls were as delicate as glass decanters, constituting the most beautiful porcelain products in the world.

Jacob also bought tasty sugar, red saffron for kidney and gastric improvement, ointments for tooth treatment, and cassia for relieving constipation. He also found indigo, alum, paper, paint, and medicinal herbs. By selling possibly only a fifth or sixth of his cargo in Alexandria market, Jacob earned enough money to surpass all the expenses he incurred while purchasing the goods. Jacob's voyage to and from Quanzhou undoubtedly proved fortunate, as he returned successfully and earned substantial profits.

闪耀在世界各地的“宋元泉州”

The Heritage of Song-Yuan Quanzhou Shining Around the World

侨居海外

Quanzhou People Living Abroad

泉州制造遍布世界

“Made-In-Quanzhou” Around the World

沉船承载的贸易史

Trade History Carried by the Sunken Ships

侨居海外

宋元泉州的繁华不只表现在刺桐港、泉州城的富庶，还有人员、物质、文化的对外交流，这体现了宋元中国影响世界的硬实力和软实力。泉州与高丽的贸易往来很频繁，引起了统治者的注意，官方层面愿意为这样的国家来往锦上添花。

据史家记载，北宋大中祥符八年（1015）至北宋元祐五年（1090），泉州到高丽的出访有 19 次，其中 16 次是商人出访，3 次是国内不得志的儒生到外国寻找机遇。当时，高丽王城内有数百华人，华人中大部分是闽人乘坐海船来到这里开展商贸活动的。高丽的统治者比较关注这些华人，或许是因为他们中的一些人接受过良好且先进的中国教育，官方层面以比较私密的方式试探他们的才能，如果发现比较合适的人才，便会提出优厚的条件，吸引他们在高丽从政，有时甚至还会强制留下一些人才，鼓励他们在高丽施展才华。泉州人刘载随商船来到高丽，在高丽睿宗时期（1105—1122）官至尚书右仆射；泉州海商欧阳征在高丽显宗时期（1009—1031）被封为谏官左右拾遗；泉州商人肖宗明在高丽文宗时期（1046—1083）被封为权知閤门祗侯。

Quanzhou People Living Abroad

The prosperity of Quanzhou during the Song and Yuan dynasties can be seen not only from the affluence of the Zayton Port and the city itself, but also from the exchanges of people, materials and culture, demonstrating the hard and soft influence of Song-Yuan China on the world. The frequent trade contacts between Quanzhou and Goryeo caught the rulers' attention, and the authorities tended to welcome and further this inter-state exchange.

As recorded in historical documents, from 1015 to 1090 during the Northern Song Dynasty, there were 19 visits from Quanzhou to Goryeo, 16 of which were made by merchants and the rest three, by scholars who found themselves nowhere in their own country and thus sought opportunities abroad. Among a few hundred Chinese inhabitants in the imperial city of Goryeo, most were Min people engaged in trade by way of sea voyages. Goryeo's rulers paid close attention to the Chinese inhabitants, probably because some of them had received good and advanced education in China. Goryeo's rulers managed to have their abilities examined in a discreet way. When suitable talents were finally spotted, some were persuaded, often with bountiful beneficial conditions, to stay and work for the Goryeo government, while others were simply detained and compelled to utilize their talent in Goryeo. They were designated as officials in Goryeo. Liu Zai from Quanzhou went to Goryeo in a merchant ship, and was assigned there as Right Deputy Imperial Clerk, a second-rank official equivalent to the prime minister during the reign of Yejong of Goryeo (1105—1122); Ouyang Zheng, a sea merchant from Quanzhou, stayed as Left and Right Censor, a supervisory official during the reign of Hyeonjong of Goryeo (1009—1031); Xiao Zongming, a Quanzhou merchant, was appointed as Imperial Secretary during the reign of Munjong of Goryeo (1046—1083).

泉州人不只在海外做官，甚至在海外创建王朝。北宋时，安南的丁琏被杀，黎威自立为王。后来，黎威亡故，安南一片混乱。当地人拥立闽人李公蕴主持时局，后来他建立了安南历史上的李氏王朝。陈日照，原名谢升卿，少年有大志，后来犯了罪，为躲避抓捕逃命在外。安南国相偶然遇到他，见他外表俊朗、才华出众，便将他带到了安南，后改名为陈日照。在安南，他尽情发挥才能，还受国相女儿倾心，结为夫妻。后来接手国事，改换李氏王朝，建立陈朝。据韩振华教授考证，判断他们是晋江安海人。他们都起始于海外贸易，最后登上王位。此外，还有很多在外的闽人航行于海上丝绸之路的宽阔海道上，他们可能名不见经传，却为商品交换和文化交融作出了巨大的贡献。

今天，当我们沿着海上丝绸之路来到东南亚、印度或阿拉伯国家时，并不会觉得太生疏，有许多事物甚至是熟悉的，或许这正是不同国家之间长期来往的结果。

位于越南首都河内的文庙，是一座典型的中国式建筑，供奉孔子。（中新图片 供图）
The Confucius Temple in Hanoi, the capital city of Vietnam, as a typical Chinese-style architecture dedicated to the worship of Confucius. (Courtesy of CNSphoto.com)

Besides holding official positions overseas, some people of Quanzhou origin even became the emperor of the dynasty they established abroad. Ly Cong Uan, for instance, enthroned by local people's acclamation, was the well-known founding emperor of the Ly Dynasty in Annam's history. This happened when Annam was in chaos at the death of its king, Le Hoan (known in Chinese documents as Li Wei), who declared himself king after his predecessor, Dinh Lien, was assassinated. Another example is an ambitious young man, Chen Rizhao, who established the Tran Dynasty to replace the Ly Dynasty. Originally named Xie Shengqing, this young man had to, allegedly, flee for his life to evade capture for the crime he had committed. His dashing good looks and outstanding talents amazed the prime minister of Annam when they met each other by chance, and he was soon taken to Annam where he brought his talents into full play and even caught the eye of the daughter of the prime minister, becoming her husband. Afterward, he undertook the state affairs. Professor Han Zhenhua found in documents evidence about their ancestral relationship with Anhai, Jinjiang in Quanzhou area, and their initial engagement in overseas trade before they eventually ascended the throne. As it was, numerous other Fujian people, lesser known as they might be, also contributed to the exchange of goods and the blending of cultures on their travel along the broad Maritime Silk Road.

Today, when people travel along the Maritime Silk Road to Southeast Asia, India, or the Arab world, things seldom look strange to them. If anything, they look familiar, perhaps because of the long history of communication between countries.

泉州制造遍布世界

府后山遗址位于泉州市区北部，据推测，该遗址应是宋代市舶司的仓库故址，距离该遗址百米处是宋代泉州府衙所在地。市舶司有抽解和榷买的职责。抽解是税收的一种方式，就是从货物中抽取一部分作为实物税，有时候是十五分之一，有时候是十分之一，也有抽解比例较大的时候。榷买就是国家垄断，专买专卖。在这一方面，官方出台法规，明确了禁止私自买卖的物品种类。市舶司为国家收购大量货物，因此要有专门的仓库来储存这些东西。

在作为市舶司仓库的府后山遗址，人们发现了大量陶瓷器，以宋元时期为主，有酱黑釉瓷、青釉瓷、青白釉瓷、素胎瓷及少量的陶器。器型丰富，有瓶、壶、砚台、碗、盘、罐、盏、盏托、器盖、碟、洗、炉、执壶、杯、灯托等。器物上有八卦纹、莲瓣纹、篦划纹、莲花纹、菊瓣纹、双鱼纹、折枝花瓣纹、缠枝花卉纹、旋转状车轮纹、篦点纹等各种纹饰。从窑口看，本地窑口产品居多，外地窑口产品也不算少。有出自本地窑，如德化窑、磁灶窑、汀溪窑、东门窑、安溪窑等的产品；也有出自外地窑，如建阳水吉窑、武夷山遇林亭窑、浙江龙泉窑、江西吉州窑、江西景德镇窑等的产品。这里明显就是一个“宋文化堆积层”。

泉州府后山遗址。（成冬冬 摄）
Fuhou Hill Site in Quanzhou. (Photo by Cheng Dongdong)

"Made-In-Quanzhou" Around the World

"Fuhou Hill Site" in the northern part of Quanzhou city is believed to be where the official warehouses of Maritime Trade Office were located, one hundred meters away from the site of the Government House of Quanzhou Prefecture in the Song Dynasty. Maritime Trade Office was responsible for levying taxes and overseeing monopolies. One way of its taxation was tax in kind, that is, a tax payable in a portion of goods, say, one-fifteenth, one-tenth, or more sometimes, and its monopolies involved buying and selling under the state control with government regulations on what products were prohibited from private trade. The Maritime Trade Office, for that matter, needed special storehouses for the large quantities of goods it acquired.

Discovered in "Fuhou Hill Site" are a great number of ceramic products glazed in brownish black, celadon or bluish white, or unglazed porcelains and a few pieces of pottery, primarily from the Song and Yuan dynasties. These vessels came in various forms like bottles, kettles, inkstones, bowls, plates, jars, tea cups known as *zhan*, tea cup stands, lids, trays, basins, stoves, handled ewers, cups, candle stands, all adorned with a variety of patterns such as eight trigrams known as *bagua*, double fish, rotating wheel, and parallel lines or dots made by fine-toothed combs. Flower patterns were also used a lot: lotus flower or its petals, chrysanthemum petals, petals from snapped branches, and flowers entwined with branches. Most were identified as products of local kilns in Dehua, Cizao, Tingxi, Dongmen, and Anxi. And there are quite a few products from places other than Quanzhou area such as Shuiji Kilns in Jianyang, Yulinting Kilns in Wuyishan, Longquan Kilns in Zhejiang, Jizhou Kilns in Jiangxi, and Jingdezhen Kilns in Jiangxi. Evidently here is "the archaeological layer of Song Culture."

在东南亚国家文莱，当代的考古学家们发现了大量遗物，其中也包含许多的瓷器残片，有出自磁灶窑、遇林亭窑、龙泉窑、景德镇窑等中国窑口的产品。这个遗址由临水居民的生活废弃物堆积而成。这些遗物与泉州府后山遗址的出土物品高度吻合。我们大致猜测，这些产品或许正是宋代从中国泉州装船运来的。这样的发现并不是偶然，海外多地都有类似的发现。

泉州磁灶窑生产的一些产品在世界各国都是热销品。比如军持，这是一种用来装水，可随身携带，又能随时净手的器物。这是专门为穆斯林地区定做的商品。又如粗瓷龙瓮，一种大大的罐子，上面有龙的纹饰盘绕瓮身，龙首、龙身、龙尾、龙爪、龙须、龙目都清晰可辨，很是鲜活。这种龙瓮风靡东南亚各国。或许正是由于瓮上龙的形象，爪哇、加里曼丹、菲律宾等地的人们把这样的瓮当作圣物代代相传。一些部落居民把它当成嫁妆，也有人把它当成死后的葬具。有的地方还会过圣瓮节。

In Brunei, a country in Southeast Asia, archaeologists discovered a large number of artifacts including numerous fragments of porcelain from kilns in different regions of China, such as Cizao Kilns, Yulinting Kilns, Longquan Kilns and Jingdezhen Kilns. This site was formed by the accumulation of discarded objects from the waterfront residents. Quite identical to the specimens found at the Fuhou Hill Site, the artifacts here are presumed to be the products shipped from Quanzhou, China during the Song Dynasty. Such discoveries are not accidental, similar products were found elsewhere in many places overseas.

Some products from Cizao Kilns in Quanzhou were highly popular around the world. Kendi, for example, a portable vessel used for holding water and for hand washing, was a commodity specially tailored for Muslim regions. Another example is the coarse porcelain loong urn, a large urn adorned with loong motifs spiraling around its body, with clear depictions of loong heads, bodies, tails, claws, mustaches, and eyes, presenting a vivid appearance. This kind of loong urn was popular in Southeast Asian countries. Perhaps it was the image of the loong on the urn that impressed people in Java, Kalimantan, and the Philippines, and they regarded such urns as sacred objects, passing them down through generations. Some tribes used them as dowries or burial articles, and in some areas, people developed a special festival to worship urns.

晋江籍华侨王奋震捐赠的海外发现的磁灶窑军持。（成冬冬 摄）

Kendi produced in Cizao Kilns, discovered overseas and donated by overseas Chinese Wang Fenzhen from Jinjiang. (Photo by Cheng Dongdong)

马可·波罗从刺桐港回到意大利时，曾随身携带一种德化生产的白瓷器。如今，在意大利威尼斯的圣马可大教堂仍能看到它们的身影。这种青白釉小罐，被一些人亲切地称为"马可·波罗罐"。

宋元泉州制造影响了世界。

"Marco Polo Jar" was a kind of white porcelain made in Dehua, Quanzhou but well-known in the world. Now housed in the Saint Mark's Basilica in Venice, Italy, this small porcelain jar with bluish-white glaze was brought to Italy from Zayton Port by Marco Polo as his personal belongings.

Everywhere in the world the influence of "Made in Quanzhou" during the Song and Yuan dynasties was strongly felt.

"南海Ⅰ号"沉船出水的宋德化窑青白釉罐，与"马可·波罗罐"器型十分相似。（段燕飞 摄）
Bluish-white glazed jars, products of Dehua Kilns in the Song Dynasty, salvaged from the "Nanhai No. 1" Shipwreck, bearing a striking resemblance to the "Marco Polo Jar." (Photo by Duan Yanfei)

沉船承载的贸易史

东行的元代新安沉船。元至治三年（1323）前后，有一艘泉州制造的海船从庆元（今浙江宁波）港出发，驶向日本福冈。不幸的是，这艘船航行到今韩国新安海域时沉没了。20 世纪七八十年代，韩国人对这艘船进行了历时九年的打捞。此次考古出土了沉船残体，发掘的文物数量惊人，多达 2.4 万余件，其中蕴藏着丰富的海洋商贸信息，有助于我们更深入地了解宋元时期的海洋贸易。

新安沉船底部龙骨连接处发现了七星伴月式的保寿孔，与 1974 年泉州发掘的宋船制作样式一致，这是泉州海船的一大特色，寓意引导海船平安航行。保寿孔内放置了七枚北宋时期的太平通宝，代表七星，另一大孔内放置了一面铜镜。令人惊异的正是这面铜镜，它不是中国生产的铜镜，而是一面产自日本的龟甲纹铜镜。有人分析，这艘船的船主或运营者是与日本关系紧密的人，他在泉州定做时要求放置这样的铜镜在龙骨内。船的样式确是福船样式，方头方尾，船甲板平衡宽大，船底却如刀刃一般尖削，既能破浪前行，又能保持平稳，船内的水密隔舱结构降低了沉没风险。作为航海利器的泉州造福船，在宋元时期或许成为外国人和定居海外的华人热衷定制、购买的产品。

太平通宝。（成冬冬 摄）
A cash coin of *Taiping Tongbao*.
(Photo by Cheng Dongdong)

Trade History Carried by the Sunken Ships

The "Xin'an" Ship of the Yuan Dynasty traveling eastward. Around 1323, a ship made in Quanzhou set sail from Qingyuan (today's Ningbo, a city in Zhejiang Province) port and headed toward Fukuoka, Japan. Unfortunately, it sank near present-day Xin'an waters in the Republic of Korea and remained buried there until 1970s and 1980s when its wreck came to light after nine years of excavation by the Republic of Korea. Behind as many as 24,000 artifacts discovered is abundant information, which improves people's understanding of the history of marine trade in the Song and Yuan dynasties.

Baoshou Holes (literally meaning "holes to maintain longevity") in the pattern of "Seven Stars around the Moon," found at the junction of the bottom keel, turned out to be a main feature of ships made in Quanzhou, as they are exactly the same as those found in the shipwreck of the Song Dynasty unearthed in 1974 in Quanzhou, which symbolized guiding the sea ships to a safe journey. Seven coins of the Northern Song Dynasty called *Taiping Tongbao* (literally meaning "peaceful currency") were placed inside the seven small holes representing seven stars while a bronze mirror was put in the large hole to stand for the Moon. Surprisingly, the mirror is not made in China but one with turtle-shell patterns produced in Japan. Such arrangement is assumed to be the special request of the ship's owner or operator who was likely to have close relations with Japan and asked that a Japanese bronze mirror be placed in the keel when the shipbuilding was commissioned in Quanzhou. With a square bow and stern, a spacious and balanced deck, a hull with a blade-like bottom that allows of both breaking waves and maintaining stability, and watertight bulkheads to reduce the risk of shipwreck, the ship indeed bears all features of a *Fu-Chuan.* As a significant sailing vessel with cutting-edge technology, *Fu-Chuan* was possibly a popular custom-made purchase among foreigners or overseas Chinese during the Song and Yuan dynasties.

新安沉船的运营者应该是在中日之间来往非常密切的人。宋元时期，日本博多有很多宋商，专门从事中日之间的海上贸易。他们之中，有人与当地人组建家庭，有人与当地的权贵和大寺庙建立了良好的联系，有人取了日语名，有人精通两国语言。日本文献中记载的“纲首”指的就是居住在博多、拥有海船并从事中日贸易的宋商。在博多出土的宋代瓷器中，能看到有许多瓷器底部书写着“王纲”“丁纲”“柳纲”等字样，这些纲首中有来自泉州的商人，他们就像在泉州的阿拉伯人联系中阿一样，联系着中日之间的海路贸易。

The operator of the Xin'an sunken ship is believed to be someone who traveled back and forth between China and Japan. Many Song merchants in Hakata, Japan, during the Song and Yuan dynasties, engaged in the marine trade between the two countries. Some of them married local people, or established good relationships with local influential people and major temples; some had both Chinese and Japanese names, and some were fluent in both languages. In Japanese literature, the term "Koshu" refers to those Song merchants who were ship owners residing in Hakata to engage in trade between Song China and Japan. Many ceramics of the Song Dynasty unearthed in Hakata have such writing on the bottom as "Wang Koshu," "Ding Koshu," "Liu Koshu," and some of these Koshu were merchants from Quanzhou. Like the Arabs who lived in Quanzhou and helped make contacts between China and the Arab world, Koshu were active connectors of maritime trade between China and Japan.

船行海上，一般要在船底放置压舱的重物。新安沉船底部放置了约27吨的铜钱，总量多达800万枚，其中大部分是中国铜钱。这些铜钱年代最早的是王莽时期的“货泉”，最晚的是元至大三年（1310）制作的至大通宝和大元通宝。中国的货币曾在日本、越南等国家的市场上流通，为当地的货币发展作出了贡献。在非洲也曾发现中国的铜钱货币。可见，宋元时期的中国货币已经具备一定的国际货币功能。当然，也有的地方可能用铜钱铸造佛像或其他工艺品。

Heavy objects were commonly used to ensure safe passage of a sailing ship at sea. Placed at the bottom of Xin'an Ship as ballast were 27 tons of copper coins, up to eight million pieces. The majority of the coins discovered are Chinese copper coins. The earliest coins found are *huo quan* introduced during the reign of Wang Mang, and the latest ones are *Zhida Tongbao* and *Dayuan Tongbao* made in 1310 in the Yuan Dynasty. Chinese coins once circulated in Japan, Vietnam, and other countries, contributing to these countries' currency development. They were also found in Africa. All this indicates that the Song-Yuan currency performed certain international monetary functions. These coins were also likely to be used to cast Buddha statues or other artifacts in some regions.

2022年6月，在中国国家博物馆“薪火赓续——罗伯昭捐赠展”上展出的“货泉”铜母范（新朝）。（中新图片 供图）

The copper coin mold of *huo quan* from the Xin Dynasty exhibited at the "Passing the Torch-Donation from Luo Bozhao" held at the National Museum of China in June 2022. (Courtesy of CNSphoto.com)

新安沉船里的产品以陶瓷器为大宗，其中有许多福建建窑、洪塘窑、义窑、德化窑、磁灶窑等窑口的产品。陶瓷器中量最大的是香炉、香瓶、香盒等香器，花瓶、花盆等花器，还有茶杯、茶壶、杯垫等茶具，可以推测日本上流社会对中国的茶道、香道和赏花之风是比较推崇的，它们已成为当时东亚地区人们的共同爱好和审美情趣。沉船中还发掘出模仿商周风格制作的青铜器，以及仿照青铜器造型制作的陶瓷器，宋人将这些器物用作香炉、食器或花瓶，这样的复古风气自然也传播到了日本和高丽，日本上层很是追捧这样的风雅之事，他们将这些器物称为“唐物”。新安沉船中还出土了许多植物类的香料药物，如胡椒、桂皮、丁香、银杏、榛子、板栗、梅子、巴豆、荔枝、使君子果、山茱萸种子等。韩国人推定这些香料大部分产于中国南部和东南亚，它们是在泉州装载的货品。元代泉州香料的进口量确实大得惊人。从新安沉船及其出土物中，我们可以看到宋元中国制造在东亚一带的流行。

新安沉船。（王峰 摄）
"Xin'an" Shipwreck. (Photo by Wang Feng)

The major commodities in the sunken ship were ceramics, many of which were from various kilns in Fujian, such as Jianyao Kilns, Hongtang Kilns, Yiyao Kilns, Dehua Kilns, and Cizao Kilns. The largest number of ceramics discovered include the typical set of three containers for incense rituals: censers, jars and boxes, as well as flower vessels like vases and pots. Still found are teacups, teapots, and coasters. These relics reveal the admiration of Japanese upper-class society for Chinese tea culture, incense ceremony, and the appreciation of flowers. They had become an interest and aesthetic taste shared by people in East Asia at that time. Also excavated from the shipwreck were bronze vessels that imitated the style of those in the Shang and Zhou dynasties (1600 B.C.—256 B.C.), and the ceramic vessels that imitated the design of bronze vessels. They were used as incense burners, tableware, or as flower vases in the Song Dynasty. This fashion of pursuing retro style had obviously spread to Japan and Goryeo. In Japan, such refined and elegant pursuits were especially favored by the upper classes, and Japanese worshiped these objects as "Tang artifacts." Also found in the Xin'an Shipwreck were various spices derived from plants, such as pepper, cinnamon, cloves, ginkgo nuts, hazelnuts, chestnuts, plums, croton seeds, lychee, quisqualis, and cornus officinalis seeds. People from the Republic of Korea speculate that most of the spices were produced in southern China and Southeast Asian regions and were loaded in Quanzhou as cargo. Indeed, the volume of imported spices in Quanzhou during the Yuan Dynasty was astonishing. The Xin'an Shipwreck and its freight do give a glimpse of the popularity of "Made in China During the Song-Yuan Period" in East Asia.

西行的南宋“南海Ⅰ号”。泉州人很早就掌握了水果腌制方法，他们从树上采摘新鲜的梅子等果实，加入食盐、沥干水分，腌制出的果子生津开胃。有一些人便把它们带到船上，用于漫漫海路的饮食所需。今天的考古学家在“南海Ⅰ号”出土物中便发现了类似的果核。有学者推测，“南海Ⅰ号”是从泉州出发的，这艘船向西南方向驶去，它的目的地是东南亚或阿拉伯地区。船上载满了瓷器、铁器，尾尖舱里也装上了许多瓷器，能装的地方全装满了。不知道是不是货物太满的原因，这艘船在广东附近的南海区域沉没了。从“南海Ⅰ号”挖掘出土的文物多达十几万件。

The "Nanhai No. 1" Shipwreck of the Southern Song Dynasty Traveling Westward. People in Quanzhou had mastered the method of fruit pickling early. They would pick fresh fruits such as plums from trees, add salt, and get them dried. Saliva-enriching and appetizing, these preserved fruits were taken aboard as a kind of dietary supplement during long sea voyages. Archaeologists have discovered pits of similar fruit on the "Nanhai No. 1" Shipwreck, and this discovery convinced some scholars that the ship might depart from Quanzhou and head southwest toward Southeast Asia or the Arab region. The ship was fully loaded with ceramics and ironware, and its stern cabin was filled with numerous ceramic items as well. All the available space was full. It is uncertain whether the cargo load played a role, but the ship sank in the vicinity of Guangdong in the South China Sea. Over 100,000 artifacts have been excavated from the "Nanhai No. 1" Shipwreck.

这艘船也是福船造型，应当是泉州制造。船上的瓷器作为商品大多是由福建德化窑、义窑、磁灶窑生产的。不寻常的是，发现于沉船左舷外侧的漆盒，应该是随船人员的私人物品，里面藏着不少宝贝，有金项链、金戒指、金制的腰带装饰品，还有标记杭州店铺信息“霸南街东王助教□”的金叶子，以及很多款有“韩四郎”字样的金叶子。这些金饰品风格迥异于南宋金器，以阿拉伯风格为主，也有宋、辽风格。金戒指一共有五枚，它们上面可能曾镶嵌着大宝石、小金饼或几颗珍珠（宝石、珍珠已遗失）。北宋时期，这样的戒指不多见。朱彧在其著作《萍洲可谈》中记录了他跟随父亲宦游的见闻，提到广州专门设置了“蕃坊”，是外国人聚居的地方，这些外国人手上都戴着镶嵌有宝石的戒指，富人戴金戒指，财力稍差的戴锡戒指，一枚质量好的戒指可能价值百金，最上等的宝石是猫眼玉石，看上去光彩熠熠、耀眼灵动。

The ship was also in the style of *Fu-Chuan*, most likely built in Quanzhou. As commodities, the majority of the ceramics on board were produced in Dehua Kilns, Yiyao Kilns, and Cizao Kilns in Fujian. The most amazing discovery is a lacquer box on the port side of the shipwreck. The box, presumably someone's personal belongings, contained various gold treasures like necklaces, rings, belt decorations, and gold leaves marked with Hangzhou store information such as "Wang Zhujiao (?), Banan Street East," and "Han Si Lang" of different styles. These gold accessories have features of both the Arabic style and the fashion of the Song and Liao dynasties, quite different from the gold artifacts in the Southern Song Dynasty. There are five gold rings in total. These gold rings are adorned with large gemstones (already missing), small gold discs, or several pearls (already missing). Such rings were not commonly found during the Northern Song Dynasty, but they are mentioned in *Pingzhou Table Talk*, a book by Zhu Yu to record his observation in his travel with his father. He noticed that in *fan fang*, quarters specially set for foreigners in Guangzhou, foreigners were wearing gem-studded rings: gold rings by the well-off and tin rings by the less wealthy. A ring of good quality might be worth about one hundred taels of gold, and the best gems were opal jade, which emanate a dazzling brilliance.

“南海Ⅰ号”出水的几条金项链也特别精致华丽，上面有莲花、卷草图案和犀角、圆环、桃实、石榴等构件，它们都是当时流行的纹样或坠饰，但项链整体结构却并非宋人惯常采用的设计，有的学者据此推测，这些器物应该是阿拉伯地区或波斯富商的私人物品，制作过程中可能有异域工匠的参与。船上还出水有一个装满果实的玻璃壶，玻璃壶用细绳捆扎，以缓冲海船摇晃带来的器物之间的碰撞。这件玻璃壶有阿拉伯风格。船上还出水有胡人雕像。因此，搭乘这艘海船的可能还有来自西亚地区和东南亚地区的外国人。

Also exquisite and splendid are several gold necklaces salvaged from the "Nanhai No. 1" Shipwreck. Designed in various patterns such as lotus and scroll grass, as well as shapes such as rhinoceros' horns, circular loops, peaches or pomegranates, these necklaces give the idea of fashion at that time. The overall structure, however, is not what Song people typically adopted. Some scholars speculate that these items were personal belongings of wealthy merchants from the Arab region or Persia, and that there might be craftsmen of foreign origin participating in the production process. Among the relics is a glass jar filled with fruits that well exhibits an Arabian style. The jar was secured with fine ropes to provide a cushion against shaking and colliding during the sea voyages. Statues of foreigners were also found in the ship, indicating that there might also be foreign individuals from West Asia and Southeast Asia on the ship.

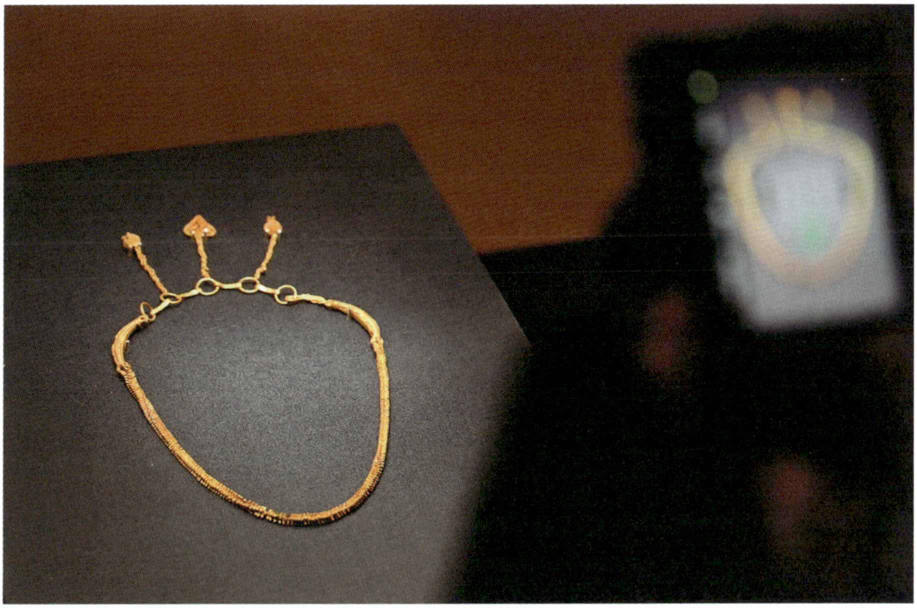

“南海Ⅰ号”沉船遗址出水的南宋时期金项链。（中新图片 供图）
The gold necklace of the Southern Song Dynasty discovered in the “Nanhai No. 1” Shipwreck. (Courtesy of CNSphoto.com)

“南海Ⅰ号”沉船遗址出水的南宋时期金叶子。（中新图片 供图）
The gold leaves of the Southern Song Dynasty discovered in the “Nanhai No. 1” Shipwreck. (Courtesy of CNSphoto.com)

“南海Ⅰ号”出水的另一种大宗商品是铁器。铁器没有放在船舱最底部，而是放在比较靠上的位置，说明它们是稍晚才装货上船的，这样对航行安全不太有利。其中有许多成捆的条状、片状的铁制品，看上去是半成品货物，有的学者认为它们是兵器坯件，因为它们呈弯刀形状。船上还出水了一些木制的柄，有一端是握把，另一端呈椭圆形，上面还有与兵器坯件对应的开孔。这些铁器可能是在中国进行初步加工的，计划等货物运到目的地后再进一步加工并组装成兵器成品，或许这也是为了绕开宋代禁止出口武器的规定。这种形制的刀不是宋代兵器风格，应是根据海外需求进行加工的订单。

无论这些推测是否正确，宋代中国的制造能力是不容置疑的。那时就已经出现根据海外客户需求进行产品生产的商业活动。这样的商业活动还有很多，比如针对阿拉伯人的金银器皿形状生产六棱形的瓷执壶，根据东南亚饮食需求生产大型盘碗。沿着海上丝绸之路向西走，中国与东南亚、中亚、非洲、欧洲国家与地区之间的交往日益密切，世界因相互交往而愈发融合。

“南海Ⅰ号”沉船遗址出水的铁条、银铤等。（段燕飞 摄）
Iron bars, silver ingots, and other items salvaged from the “Nanhai No. 1” Shipwreck. (Photo by Duan Yanfei)

Another major commodity discovered in the "Nanhai No. 1" Shipwreck was ironware. Placed in a relatively higher position of the ship's hold rather than at the bottom, the ironware was assumed to be loaded onto the ship at a later time. This arrangement was considered unfavorable for the ship's stability at sea. There are many iron products in bundled bars and sheets, which seemed to be semi-finished products. Some scholars believe that they are spare parts of unfinished weapons, because they are in the shape of curved blades. Also recovered were several wooden handles, with one end serving as a grip and the other end, oval-shaped, with corresponding holes for the weapon components. It is likely that they were initially made in China, and were supposed to be further processed and assembled into weapons at their destination. Perhaps this was done to circumvent Song court's prohibition on the outflow of weapons. Bearing no resemblance to the style of the weapons of the Song Dynasty, these blade forms were perhaps produced based on overseas demand.

Regardless of the accuracy of the speculations, The strong manufacturing ability of China during the Song Dynasty was undeniable. There was already bespoke service in goods production to cater to overseas customers, and quite a lot of such commercial activities were organized. For example, hexagonal porcelain kettles were modeled after the Arabic designs of gold and silver wares; large plates and bowls were tailored to meet the dietary needs from people in Southeast Asia. Traveling westward along the Maritime Silk Road, China developed closer communication with countries and regions in Southeast Asia, Central Asia, Africa, and Europe. Encounters as such brought the world closer together.

宋元泉州的魅力渊源

The Driving Force Behind Song-Yuan Quanzhou's Charm

泉州人稠山谷瘠，虽欲就耕无处辟

A Populous City with Limited Land to Till

州南有海浩无穷，每岁造舟通异域

A Shipbuilding Place with Limitless Access to the Sea

有这样一个现象，也许能从一个侧面印证宋元时期泉州的“国际范”：当时，许多波斯、阿拉伯等地的穆斯林慕名来到泉州，一些家族在此定居——在宋元历史上发挥重要作用的蒲氏家族，南宋时举家从广州迁往泉州；泉州两大回族家族——丁氏、郭氏，他们的先祖也正是在宋元时期来到泉州。他们为什么在这段时间不谋而合迁入泉州？各个家族的迁徙是偶然事件，但偶然背后一定藏着共同的必然因素。

宋元泉州究竟有什么样的魅力，以至于深深吸引着五湖四海的经商者呢？为何是宋元泉州？学者们一直在寻找答案，各种答案也都各有道理。

Quanzhou's "International Fame" during the Song and Yuan dynasties can be circumstantially evidenced by the migration of many Muslims of Persian or Arabian origin who were attracted to Quanzhou by its reputation. Some families settled here. The Pu Family that played an important part during the Song-Yuan period moved from Guangzhou to Quanzhou in the Southern Song Dynasty; the ancestors of the Ding Family and the Guo Family, two prominent Hui families in Quanzhou, also came to Quanzhou during the Song-Yuan period. Their coincidental migration into Quanzhou at that period can be attributable to the respective chance events in their family's relocation, but still something in common lying behind and arguably inevitable should be factored in.

What exactly drew merchants from all over the world to Song-Yuan Quanzhou? Why was Quanzhou their destination? Scholars have been trying hard to find answers, yet answers vary and each has its own reasoning.

陈埭丁氏宗祠。（成冬冬 摄）

Ancestral Hall of Ding Family in Chendai Town, Jinjiang, Quanzhou. (Photo by Cheng Dongdong)

百奇郭氏家庙祀祖典仪。（成冬冬 摄）

Ancestors worshiping ceremony held in the Ancestral Hall of Guo Family in Baiqi Village, Quanzhou. (Photo by Cheng Dongdong)

泉州优良的港湾等自然地理条件，稳定和平的社会环境，适合农贸经济作物生长的气候，丰富的铁矿、瓷土和木材等资源，都成为宋元泉州发展繁荣的重要因素。宋金战争期间，泉州不受纷扰，获得了加速发展的机遇，泉州的商贸地位从此更加突出。宋朝廷南迁，也是一个极其重要的因素，泉州从来没有像这个时候距离中国的政治中心如此近便。元朝官方给予泉州的政策优势、泉州造船业兴旺发达等因素，也都受到学者重视……

港口城市发展的因素是相似的，良好的地理条件、优秀的制造能力是基础，但能否在此基础上兼得明智的治理、开明的政策和完美的历史机遇，这与运气多少有几分关系，而泉州的崛起正是恰逢天时、地利与人和。

Here is a list of important factors that contributed to the prosperity of Song-Yuan Quanzhou: favorable natural and geographic conditions such as its excellent ports and bays, a stable and peaceful social environment, a climate suitable for growing cash crops for agricultural trade, as well as abundant iron ore, porcelain clay, and timber. During the Song-Jin War (1125—1234), Quanzhou remained undisturbed, thereby gaining the chance of accelerated development. They city's importance in trade and commerce was highlighted. Another significant factor was the relocation of the Song court to the south: never before had Quanzhou been so close to the political center of China. Other considerations like the preferential policies from the authorities and the flourishing shipbuilding industry in Quanzhou have also received scholarly attention.

Factors contributing to the development of a port city are more or less similar: advantageous geographic conditions and remarkable manufacturing capacities as solid foundations. However, wise governance, correct policies, and right historical opportunities, and sometimes luck too, all play a role. The rise of Quanzhou was a result of opportune time, geographic advantage, and concerted efforts on the part of its people.

泉州人稠山谷瘠，虽欲就耕无处辟

宋代谢履写过一首《泉南歌》:“泉州人稠山谷瘠，虽欲就耕无处辟。州南有海浩无穷，每岁造舟通异域。”这是对当时泉州自然与人文环境的客观呈现，其中也藏着泉州成为宋元中国的世界海洋商贸中心的原因。

泉州多山，山区有茂密的森林资源，山与山之间是平原，河流穿越平原、滋养土壤，可以种植大量的粮食、蔬菜和经济作物；沿海可产出丰富的海盐、海鲜。泉州人依靠山海而谋生，在适应自然、改造自然的过程中繁衍生息。正是这样一片土地吸引了一代又一代从北方到来的移居者。

A Populous City with Limited Land to Till

"Quanzhou, a populous city with not much fertile land to till, but a sea in the south vast enough; each year locally built ships traveled far to the foreign lands." Such was a real picture of the natural and cultural environment of Quanzhou at that time captured in *Song of Quanzhou* by Xie Lyu in the Song Dynasty. This poem reveals the reasons why Quanzhou became the world maritime trade center during the Song and Yuan dynasties.

Sitting among mountains, Quanzhou was home to rich forest resources, and had plains with rivers flowing through to nourish the soil. The land was suitable for the cultivation of a large number of crops, vegetables and cash crops. With abundant forest resources in the mountainous region and great amount of sea salt and sea food in the coastal areas, its mountains and the sea alone provided reliance for Quanzhou people who lived and thrived as they were adapting themselves to and changing the nature. Such was the land that attracted generations of people from the north.

随着人口日益增长，原本丰厚的山海资源便显得紧张。唐开元年间，泉州人口增长至三万七千零五十四户。北宋初年，泉州人口已达八九万户。北宋元丰年间，泉州人口已超过二十万户，占福建总人口的20%以上，而泉州土地面积却只占福建土地总面积的9%。南宋后期，泉州人口又增长至二十五万户。这么狭小的一片土地又怎能满足如此众多人口的需求？泉州的土地越来越稀缺。泉州人不得不挖山垦地，不得不围海造田。终于在无地可辟的情况下，泉州人开始打破旧的思路，寻找这片土地的另一种可能。

But the rich mountain and sea resources were later reduced under the pressure of ever increasing number of people. For example, population in Quanzhou rose to 37,054 households during the Kaiyuan period (713—741) of the Tang Dynasty, and about 80,000 or 90,000 during the early years of the Northern Song Dynasty. During the Yuanfeng period (1078—1085) of the Northern Song Dynasty, its population had exceeded 200,000 households, accounting for more than 20% of the population of Fujian Province while its land area took up only 9% of the whole province. It continued to grow to 250,000 households in the late years of the Southern Song Dynasty. How could such a small piece of land satisfy the need from a huge number of people? The growing population made lands in Quanzhou scarcer and local people had to reclaim land from mountains and the sea. When there were no more lands left to develop, Quanzhou people began to think outside the box and managed to explore other possibilities on this land.

他们转向了工商业，从事纺织、制瓷、矿冶、造船、酿酒、煮糖、造纸、印刷等行业。他们想办法把这些商品以及中国其他地方的商品销售到海外，并将海外的商品转运销售到国内和其他国家，发展外贸和转口贸易。大量的商人、销售员涌现出来，还有船长、水手等各个工作岗位也都需要人手，这就促进了就业，拓展了人们的谋生之路。之后，人们用挣得的财富采购食物、建设城市，这样相辅相成、良性循环，城市也更加繁荣了。

独特的地理环境和人口状况塑造了泉州人向海发展的思路，即便他们的祖上并没有以海为生的经验，谋生的强烈需求也会催促着他们鼓起勇气面向大海，敢于冒险，不断开拓，这也正是宋元泉州发展繁荣的动力之源，这种精神融于泉州人的血脉之中，延续至今。

The breakthrough they made was to turn to industry and commerce. Engaged in industries such as textiles, ceramics, mining and metallurgy, shipbuilding, brewing, sugar production, papermaking, and printing, they also participated in foreign trade, selling products of those industries as well as goods from other parts of China to overseas markets. While distributing and selling foreign goods to domestic markets and other countries, they came to be involved in entrepot trade. A great number of traders and peddlers emerged, and demand for personnel like captains and sailors grew, resulting in a boost in employment, and more secured means of living. Soon people used the wealth they earned to buy sustenance and build their own city, creating a more prosperous city where people found their living conditions and the city construction in line with each other.

It is the particular geographical conditions and the demographic situation that steered the development of Quanzhou toward the sea. Even when there was hardly any experience Quanzhou people could learn from their ancestors, their urge to earn a living was so strong that they plucked up the courage to pilot their boats into the sea. This daring spirit of working hard to explore flowing in Quanzhou people's vein, became the driving force behind the growth of Quanzhou during the Song and Yuan dynasties and it still works today.

州南有海浩无穷，每岁造舟通异域

当泉州人用商贸连通世界，世界便成为支持他们成长的力量。雅各在泉州时曾见证了商人阶层的崛起，他认为泉州是一座以商贸为主的城市，权力阶层中已有商业的影响，这样的氛围也作用于贵族阶层和士人阶层。南宋刘克庄有诗云：“闽人务本亦知书，若不耕樵必业儒。惟有桐城南郭外，朝为原宪暮陶朱。”意思是说，福建人是守本分的，也热爱读书，在耕田砍樵的间隙，一定会像儒生一样奋发图强、耕读传家。但是刺桐城南外围却是一个例外，那里的人早上希望像孔子的弟子原宪一样以儒为业，晚上却又希望像陶朱公范蠡一样营商。

德济门是宋元泉州城市南部商业性城区的重要地标。（吴志诚 摄）
Deji Gate, an important landmark of the southern commercial area of Quanzhou city in the Song and Yuan dynasties. (Photo by Wu Zhicheng)

A Shipbuilding Place with Limitless Access to the Sea

The world seemed to people of Quanzhou a place to support their growth when they found that trade could be a bridge to connect the world. In Quanzhou, there soon arose a merchant class, as witnessed by Jacob who believed that the city had become primarily commercial and there in the ruling class existed the influence of commerce. Such atmosphere also affected the nobility and the scholar class, as can be seen from a poem by Liu Kezhuang, a poet in the Southern Song Dynasty. According to the poem, Min people valued both farming and pursuit of learning and knowledge, and if not engaged in farm cultivation or woodcutting, they would surely work on Confucian classics to become a scholar, as was a tradition most families hoped to establish and pass on. But there was an exception in the business center in the south of Quanzhou where its residents were said to follow the scholarly pursuit like Yuan Xian, one of Confucius' students, in the morning, while in the evening, their aspiration shifted to what Fan Li, the ancient Chinese sage of business, also known by the name Tao Zhu Gong, advocated about the importance of trade activities.

宋元泉州的社会结构不同于传统，是以工商业为主体，农业为辅助的。宋代福建的盐场有 303 处，泉州就占了 294 处。据记载，每年因营盐失当而受刑狱的人就有数万人。包括铜、银、铁等在内的冶矿行业从业者当时应该也有万人以上。泉州瓷窑众多，规模大，窑工也不计其数。此外，宋元泉州的造船业也很发达，极盛时有海舶 1.5 万艘之多。元军出海征战，委托泉州制造了大量的海船，泉州也常常作为重要的出发港。而支撑这样规模船舶需求的背后又是多少工匠的辛勤劳动！

Differing from the past, the social structure of Quanzhou during the Song and Yuan dynasties was based on industry and commerce, with agriculture only as a supplement. In salt industry, for example, out of 303 salt fields in Fujian, 294 were in Quanzhou. Each year, tens of thousands of people were put into prison for their mismanagement of the salt business. Industry of copper, silver, and iron mining and smelting required over ten thousand of practitioners. Numerous large-scale porcelain kilns in Quanzhou also necessitated an uncountable number of kiln workers. Besides, the shipbuilding industry here was very advanced during the Song and Yuan dynasties, and more than 15,000 ships were built in its heyday. The city was not only a place to be entrusted with the task of building a large quantity of warships by the Yuan army for sea battles, but also an important departure port. Still to be mentioned and given credit were the countless craftsmen who toiled and moiled to meet the great demand of ships of this scale.

辛勤劳作的盐工。（陈英杰 摄）
Industrious salt workers. (Photo by Chen Yingjie)

泉州海外交通史博物馆内的福船建造场景。（段燕飞 摄）
Fu-Chuan construction scene inside Quanzhou Maritime Museum. (Photo by Duan Yanfei)

今天我们能看到的泉州宋元时期的古沉船有很多，船上出土文物数量也很惊人，可以想象当时从泉州出发、驶向大海冒险求财的场面必定是帆影幢幢、人声鼎沸。即便赴海经营是九死一生，但若有幸安然无恙，所能挣得的利润足以保证生活富有，因此，人们前赴后继，投身于海上贸易。向海外异域求索不仅充实了泉州的财富，也重新塑造了泉州人的性格。因此，泉州人不只有对“天”的追求，以成为天子门生为荣，还有对“海”的无穷遐想，海外的金山银山也令人流连忘返。

Today standing in front of the numerous ancient ship remains and the staggering number of excavated artifacts of the Song and Yuan dynasties, one can easily picture a busy port of Song-Yuan Quanzhou, where countless junks, upon their departure, thronged the water jostling their sails over the hubbub. On the swaying boats were people who never wavered in their decision to take a chance to have their fortune made on the other side of the sea. For all the life-threatening risks these overseas voyages might entail, the massive irresistible profits never failed to tempt the audacious men, one after another, to venture into sea, hoping that they could return safe and sound, with a fortune big enough to secure an affluent life. As a result, Quanzhou people continuously dedicated themselves to the overseas trade. In return, the overseas exploration built for the city not only its wealth but new character as well. For that matter, people of Song-Yuan Quanzhou not only pursued the "heaven" hoping to be chosen by the emperor in the imperial examination, but also cast their endless desires over the sea, hoping to reach the land that they believed was paved with gold and silver.

泉州宋元遗产的启示

Legacies of Song-Yuan Quanzhou

公元 10—14 世纪的宋元泉州，创造了一个东方文明神话，她创造性地让农耕文明和商业文明在中国东南产生碰撞、和谐共融。管理者合理的措施和开放的态度促进了中国海洋文明的发展，使宋元中国成为世界的生产、销售、运输基地和枢纽。世界各地不乏重要的港口和贸易城市，它们各自拥有特色产业和贸易优势，却几乎没有哪个城市像宋元泉州一样具备如此全面的制造能力和巨大的贸易规模。中国生产了大量的瓷器、铁器，商品销售范围涵盖了东亚地区、东南亚地区、阿拉伯地区、欧洲地区和非洲地区。宋元中国既是世界贸易体系的发动机，也是主要的消费者。泉州是宋元中国的一个窗口和代表，她向内融合中原文明，向外闯荡海洋、沟通世界，成为那个时代一道亮丽的风景线。

这是一个整体和谐、文明、多元的历史时期，人们因贸易而相聚，进行商品生产、交换和运输，没有谁因种族、国家而对他人怀有敌意，也没有谁开展灭绝人性、奴役掠夺式的商业活动。这是中国为世界打造的 10—14 世纪的海上丝绸之路贸易活动，它具有世界性的历史和现实意义。宋元之后，泉州的很多事物逐渐湮灭于历史之中，世界也经历了许多次重大的变革和发展。站在当今回看宋元泉州，它让我们窥见中国文明里蕴藏的包容、和平与智慧，世界海洋贸易依然需要“和而不同，美美与共”的思想。

宋元虽已逝，但在泉州的大地上还保留着许多珍贵的文化遗产。这些遗产组成“泉州：宋元中国的世界海洋商贸中心”系列，共同向世界宣告它们所具有的突出的普遍价值。这 22 处世界遗产分为四组：

第一组是体现制度保障的九日山祈风石刻、市舶司遗址、德济门遗址、天后宫、真武庙。九日山祈风石刻记载了宋朝官员为海商举办祈风仪式的详细情况，体现了国家对海洋贸易的重视；市舶司曾是管理海外贸易业务的官方办公机构；德济门曾是泉州城南商业宝地的重要地标；天后宫体现了妈祖信俗之于海洋贸易发展的重要意义，宫内供奉着成神于民间、又不断被官方加封的林默娘；真武庙也曾是官方祭祀海神的重要场所。

Song-Yuan Quanzhou during the 10th to 14th centuries is believed to have created a myth of Eastern civilization, where the collision of agriculture and commerce ingeniously led to a harmonious integration in Southeast China. The administrators' reasonable measures and open attitudes accelerated the evolution of Chinese maritime civilization, making Song-Yuan China a global hub of production, sales and transportation. While there were many other important ports and commercial cities in the world noted for their own specialty industries and commercial advantages, none possessed the comprehensive capabilities and great trade scale of Song-Yuan Quanzhou. When a stunning number of made-in-China products like porcelains and ironware were sold in East Asia, Southeast Asia, the Arab world, Europe, and Africa, China amazed the world as an engine as well as a major consumer in the global trade system. Quanzhou, representing Song-Yuan China, was a place that absorbed the domestic culture of the Central Plains and ventured out into the ocean to connect the world, creating quite a sight to behold in the era.

In this age characterized by a holistic perception of harmony, civilization and diversity, people gathered for the sake of trade—commodity production, exchange and transportation—with neither discrimination based on race or nationality, nor commercial activities for any inhumane or predatory purposes. These trade events rolling out on the Maritime Silk Road initiated by China during the 10th to 14th centuries carried worldwide historical significance and are still relevant today. Although much of Song-Yuan Quanzhou had fallen into oblivion since a long passage of time from the conclusion of the Song and Yuan dynasties, and the world also underwent its dramatic changes and developments, our present look back at the city still enables us to catch a glimpse of inclusiveness, peace and wisdom embedded in Chinese civilization, and to come to understand that the principle of "harmony in diversity" still holds true in global maritime trade today.

Days of Song-Yuan period were gone, yet many of its precious cultural heritages have endured to today in Quanzhou city, constituting the world heritage series of "Quanzhou: Emporium of the World in Song-Yuan China." The 22 sites together proclaimed to the world their outstanding universal value. The following are the four categories of these world heritage sites.

The first are the sites of institutional guarantee that include Jiuri Mountain Wind-Praying Inscriptions, Site of Maritime Trade Office, Site of Deji Gate, Tianhou Temple and Zhenwu Temple. Jiuri Mountain Wind-Praying Inscriptions recorded the details of ceremonial venue where Song officials used to pray for propitious winds and good luck for sea merchants, reflecting the great official support for maritime trade. Maritime Trade Office was an administrative office to deal with overseas trade. Deji Gate was an important landmark in the commercial center on the southern side of Quanzhou city. Tianhou Temple was a manifestation of the importance of Mazu belief and customs to the development of overseas trade. Enshrined here is a Chinese sea goddess, Lin Moniang, who was initially deified by common people and later conferred with official titles by governments many times. Zhenwu Temple was also an important venue to worship sea gods officially.

石狮红塔湾，潮起美如斯。（陈起拓 摄）
Spectacular tides at Hongta Bay in Shishi, Quanzhou. (Photo by Chen Qituo)

第二组是体现多元社群的南外宗正司遗址、泉州文庙及学宫、开元寺、老君岩造像、清净寺、伊斯兰教圣墓、草庵摩尼光佛造像。南外宗正司是宋代南迁泉州的皇族群体的管理机构，这一群体既参与海外贸易，也是海外奢侈品的重要消费者；泉州文庙是纪念和祭祀儒家思想创始人孔子的场所，学宫是培养儒学学子的地方，曾为国家培养了许多栋梁之材；开元寺、老君岩造像分别与佛教信仰和道教信仰有关，宋元泉州的僧侣也积极参与到了城市基础设施建设和港口贸易中；清净寺、伊斯兰教圣墓体现了穆斯林群体在泉州的重要作用，他们是沟通中外贸易的重要群体。

Sites of the second group hint a culture of diversified communities that consist of Site of Southern Clan Office, Confucius Temple and School, Kaiyuan Temple, Statue of Lao Tze, Qingjing Mosque, Islamic Tombs, and Statue of Mani in Cao'an Temple. Southern Clan Office was the administrative institution for the imperial descendants of the Song Dynasty who, after moving southward to Quanzhou, became involved in maritime trade and were the important consumers of luxury goods from abroad. Confucius Temple was the place to commemorate and worship Confucius, founder of the philosophy known as Confucianism, and the School was established to nurture talents, many of whom later became the backbone of the nation. Kaiyuan Temple and Statue of Lao Tze related to Buddhism and Taoism respectively witnessed their religious members' active role in urban infrastructure construction and port trade. Qingjing Mosque and Islamic Tombs bespoke the significant contributions Muslims had made in Quanzhou: they were the important people to facilitate the trade between China and foreign countries.

第三组是作为商品产地的磁灶窑址（金交椅山窑址）、德化窑址（尾林—内坂窑址、屈斗宫窑址）、安溪青阳下草埔冶铁遗址。它们是商品生产基地的重要代表，宋元泉州的相关遗址还有很多。

第四组是构成交通运输网络的洛阳桥、安平桥、顺济桥遗址、江口码头、石湖码头、六胜塔、万寿塔。几座桥为运输带来巨大便利，完善了商品交易网络，这是交通与贸易相互依存、良性发展的结果；六胜塔、万寿塔是重要的航标塔，曾有许多针路簿是以泉州为中心展开规划与叙述的。

这一系列世界文化遗产从泉州沿海一直延伸到内陆腹地，有的在海边，有的在河口，有的在城内，有的在山里。宋元时代的发展对泉州全域的推动和改变是巨大的。四组文化遗产相互依托，共同成就了超出单个个体意义叠加的总和，使“泉州：宋元中国的世界海洋商贸中心”成为世界遗产体系的又一个具有创新性的系列遗产范本。泉州的 22 处世界遗产点向世人揭示了人类曾经成就的另一种海洋商贸典范，对如今的海陆发展具有重要的实践、思想和精神意义。

On the list of the third category are representatives of the important commodity production bases: Sites of Cizao Kilns (Jinjiaoyishan Kilns), Sites of Dehua Kilns (Weilin-Neiban Kilns and Qudougong Kiln), Xiacaopu Iron Production Site of Qingyang Village in Anxi, to name just a few.

Listed as the fourth category are sites of transportation networks: Luoyang Bridge, Anping Bridge, Site of Shunji Bridge, Estuary Docks, Shihu Dock, Liusheng Pagoda, and Wanshou Pagoda. Construction of these bridges greatly facilitated transportation and improved the trading network system, showing the interdependence of transportation and trade and their sound development. The two pagodas were once so important as navigation towers that many books of sailing directions, also known as *zhen lu bu* in Chinese, would take Quanzhou as the center to plan and explain voyage routes.

The heritages are distributed from the coastal areas of Quanzhou to the inland hinterland, some along the coast, some at the river mouth, others within the city, and still others in the mountains. The development during the Song and Yuan dynasties propelled the city of Quanzhou into a dramatic transformation in every aspect. The interconnection and interdependence between the four categories shape a holistic significance that goes beyond the meaning of its individual parts, making this project of "Quanzhou: Emporium of the World in Song-Yuan China" an innovative serial heritage model within the World Heritage system. The 22 world heritage sites in Quanzhou reveal to the world another trade paradigm of maritime commerce humanity once possessed, and they still make sense in today's development of land and sea in terms of its practice, idea and spirit.

宋元泉州的历史也能给我们带来许多启发。泉州发展了一千多年，才取得了极辉煌极壮丽的成就，但元末持续数年的动荡不安，使这来之不易的发展积淀遭受重创。战乱对城市的影响是巨大的。因此，我们应当热爱和平、珍惜生活。

泉州崛起的过程也比较缓慢，它是中国开发较晚的地区之一，经历了几个朝代的建设才达到足以与其他城市匹敌的生产制造、造船航海水平。每个城市都要坚持发展、面向未来，否则即便有再好的机遇也都是枉然。泉州在发展的过程中，不断向海求地，晋江、洛阳江两岸的一些土地也被人们占用，使得今天泉州的江面已经远远小于过去。出现这样的情况，既有自然原因，也有人为原因。倘若我们在寻求发展的同时多加爱惜哺育我们的生态环境，大江大河才能更好地发挥运输和停泊功能，才能实现城市的可持续发展。

晋江出海口。（陈英杰 摄）
Estuary of the Jinjiang River. (Photo by Chen Yingjie)

The history of Song-Yuan Quanzhou is enlightening. It took more than one thousand years for Quanzhou to achieve its spectacular success, but the turmoil that lasted for years at the end of the Yuan Dynasty caused immense damage to the hard-earned achievements. To avoid the ravages of wars that are always ruinous to a city, we are duty bound to defend and maintain peace and cherish our life.

The gradual rise of Quanzhou is full of implications. After generations of construction efforts in many dynasties, the city grew from a district that was relatively late to begin its development to a city that could compete with other cities in its capabilities of production and manufacturing, shipbuilding and seafaring. Its success suggests the importance of persistence in development and looking forward to the future, without which even the best chance would bear no fruits. In the process of Quanzhou's growth, people have continuously managed to reclaim lands from the ocean. Their exploitation of the lands on both banks of the Jinjiang River and the Luoyang River has caused the reduction of the river area in the city. The occurrence of such situations is due to both natural and human factors. If we take care of the ecological environment while seeking development, the rivers can better serve their functions of transportation and anchorage, enabling sustainable urban development.

宋元泉州的商业繁荣也与官方所持态度有关。宋代比其他中国古代历史朝代更加鼓励工商业，宋代的军事实力或许不是最强的，但所创造的物质和精神财富却熠熠生辉。官方施以有力的制度保障，为民间贸易注入活力，始终坚持开放、包容，市场环境相对自由、宽松。

商贸繁荣，还需要参与者讲信誉、敢拼搏。对于泉州来说，宋元海贸盛景已成为历史，但那个时代所孕育的商业精神却被一代代闽南人承袭下来，或许这就是泉州世界文化遗产最宝贵的价值，流淌在每一个闽南人的血液里。

泉州海外交通史博物馆外的福船模型。（成冬冬　摄）
The *Fu-Chuan* model outside Quanzhou Maritime Museum. (Photo by Cheng Dongdong)

The business boom in Song-Yuan Quanzhou is also indicative of the attitude the government adopted. Compared with governments of other dynasties in ancient China, the Song government gave more support to the official advocacy of industry and commerce, leading to the nation's brilliantly impressive accumulation of material and cultural wealth, irrespective of its perhaps not the strongest military strength. It is the government's firm institutional guarantee that injected vitality into private trade, secured an air of openness and inclusiveness, and ensured a relatively free and tolerant market environment.

Last but not least, commercial vibrancy would not have been possible without participants' trustworthiness and their daring to struggle. These business legacies, to the people of Quanzhou, have never been lost with the bygone glory of overseas trade during the Song-Yuan period; instead, they have been well preserved and passed on among people in southern Fujian from generation to generation. Perhaps these are the invaluable cultural heritage Quanzhou has contributed to the world and they keep running deep in the hearts of its people.

参考文献

[1] 陈筱 . 泉州城市历史地理初探 [J]. 海交史研究 ,1995(02):90—97.

[2] 许清泉 , 王洪涛 . 福建晋江流域丰州地区考古调查 [J]. 考古 ,1961(04):193+221.

[3] 林汀水 . 泉州地理环境变迁与泉州田野风光旅游 [J]. 闽都文化研究 ,2004(01):253—259.

[4] 泉州古港史编写委员会 . 泉州古港史 [M]. 北京 : 人民交通出版社 ,1994.

[5] 中国海外交通史研究会 , 福建省泉州海外交通史博物馆 . 泉州海外交通史料汇编 [M]. 泉州 :[出版者不详],1983.

[6] 汤漳平 . 河洛文化与闽南文化综论 [M]. 郑州 : 河南人民出版社 ,2018.

[7] 蔡保全 . 从贝丘遗址看福建沿海先民的居住环境与资源开发 [J]. 厦门大学学报（哲学社会科学版）,1998(03):106—111.

[8] 余海涛 . 泉州“南安四贤”史迹研究 [J]. 西安文理学院学报（社会科学版）,2019,22(01):68—74.

[9] 庄锦清 , 林华东 . 福建南安大盈出土青铜器 [J]. 考古 ,1977(03):169−172.

[10] 吕荣芳 . 对福建南安大盈出土青铜器的几点看法 [J]. 考古 ,1978(05):319—320+337.

[11] 吴艺娟 . 南安丰州成为六朝时期闽南政治、经济中心的原因——以六朝古墓葬考古发掘为例 [J]. 四川文物 ,2008(03):79—83.

[12] 陈建中 . 泉州南安丰州六朝墓群出土“阮”纹砖及其学术意义初探 [J]. 东南文化 ,2007(03):37—40+101.

[13] 林宗鸿 . 泉州开元寺发现五代石经幢等重要文物 [J]. 泉州文史 ,1986(9):29—32.

[14] 李玉昆 , 李秀梅 . 泉州古代海外交通史 [M]. 北京 : 中国广播电视出版社 ,2006.

[15] 泉州市地方志编纂委员会 . 历史名城泉州 [M]. 福州 : 海风出版社 ,2007.

[16] 吴泰 , 陈高华 . 宋元时期的海外贸易和泉州港的兴衰 [J]. 海交史研究 ,1978(00):5—16.

[17] 童家洲 . 试论宋元泉州港繁盛的原因 [J]. 文史哲 , 1980(4):58—65.

[18] 李军 . 宋元“海上丝绸之路”繁荣时期广州、明州（宁波）、泉州三大港口发展之比较研究 [J]. 南方文物 ,2005(01):76—82.

[19] 梁二平 . 宋元大港杭州、泉州的海上风光 [J]. 丝绸之路 ,2015(23):1—7.

[20] 杨文新 . 宋代南外宗正司入闽及其影响 [J]. 史学月刊 ,2004(08):25—29.

[21] 黄伟 . 泉州南外宗赵氏源流 [J]. 闽台缘 ,2018(2):69—75.

[22] 桑原骘藏 . 蒲寿庚考 [M]. 北京 : 中华书局 ,2009.

[23] 吴幼雄 . 宋代泉州汪、真两郡守的改革及社会效果 [J]. 泉州师范学院学报 , 1988(1):80—86.

[24] 蒋颖贤 . 真德秀与泉州海外贸易 [J]. 海交史研究 ,1982(00):120—126.

[25] 陈桂炳 . 元末偰玉立治泉州事迹钩沉 [J]. 乌鲁木齐职业大学学报 , 2001(1):50—54.

[26] 泉州市地方志编纂委员会 . 外国人在泉州与泉州人在海外 [M]. 福州 : 海风出版社 ,2007.
[27] 陈高华 . 印度马八儿王子孛哈里来华新考 [J]. 南开学报（哲学社会科学版）,1980(4):70—73.
[28] 汪大渊著 , 苏继庼校释 . 岛夷志略校释 [M]. 北京 : 中华书局 ,1981.
[29] 赵汝适著 , 杨博文校释 . 诸蕃志校释 [M]. 北京 : 中华书局 ,2000.
[30] 庄为玑 , 庄景辉 . 泉州宋船木牌木签考释 [J]. 厦门大学学报（哲学社会科学版）,1980(01):64—71.
[31] 吴鸿洲 . 泉州出土宋海船所载香料药物考 [J]. 浙江中医学院学报 ,1981(03):44—47.
[32] 夏时华 . 宋代市舶香药纲运考述 [J]. 云南社会科学 ,2015(06):158—164.
[33] 李玉昆 . 宋元时期泉州的香料贸易 [J]. 海交史研究 ,1998(01):58—67.
[34] 栗建安 . 世界遗产视野下的泉州古窑址考古与研究 [J]. 自然与文化遗产研究 ,2021,6(03):40—47.
[35] 李知宴 , 陈鹏 . 宋元时期泉州港的陶瓷输出 [J]. 海交史研究 ,1984(00):39—48.
[36] 陈丽芳 . 从水下考古发现看德化宋元时期外销瓷 [C]// 中国古陶瓷学会 , 厦门市博物馆 , 泉州市博物馆 . 福建陶瓷与海上丝绸之路：中国古陶瓷学会福建会员大会暨研讨会论文集 . 长春 : 东北师范大学出版社 ,2016:101—112.
[37] 德安科纳 . 光明之城 [M]. 塞尔本 , 编译 . 杨民 , 程钢 , 刘国忠 , 等 , 译 . 上海 : 上海人民出版社 ,1999.
[38] 沙海昂 , 注 . 冯承钧 , 译 . 马可波罗行纪 [M]. 上海 : 上海古籍出版社 ,2014.
[39] 白图泰 . 伊本・白图泰游记 [M]. 马金鹏 , 译 . 北京 : 华文出版社 ,2015.
[40] 韩振华 . 中国与东南亚关系史研究 [M]. 南宁 : 广西人民出版社 ,1992:97—100.
[41] 傅恩凤 . 泉州府后山遗址与文莱甜桔子河遗址出土瓷器之分析 [J]. 福建文博 ,2019(02):69—73.
[42] 贾志扬 . 宋代与东亚的多国体系及贸易世界 [J]. 北京大学学报（哲学社会科学版）,2009,46(02):99—108.
[43] 金英美 . 新安沉船：韩国海域里的“中国制造”[J]. 美成在久 ,2018(01):6—15.
[44] 范佳楠 . 新安沉船与 14 世纪的中日海上贸易 [J]. 自然与文化遗产研究 ,2019,4(10):21−27.
[45] 赵志军 . 宋代远洋贸易商船“南海一号”出土植物遗存 [J]. 农业考古 ,2018(03):7—17.
[46] 杨睿 .“南海 I 号”南宋沉船若干问题考辨 [J]. 博物院 ,2018(02):27—32.
[47] 李岩 . 南海 I 号里的镶嵌宝石黄金首饰 [J]. 美成在久 ,2020(02):6—25.
[48] 田国敏 . 马可・波罗“南海 I 号”德化窑瓷 [J]. 文物天地 ,2020(02):23—24.

[49] 冯正腾 . “南海 I 号”瓷器反映的多文化融合 [J]. 文物天地 ,2020(02):61—63.

[50] 廖大珂 . 宋元时期泉州的阿拉伯人 [J]. 回族研究 ,2011(2):21—30.

[51] 王四达 . 宋元泉州港繁荣原因新探 [J]. 华侨大学学报（哲学社会科学版）,1989(02):63—71+46.

[52] 王四达 . 宋元泉州的社会转型及其文化特征初探 [J]. 华侨大学学报（哲学社会科学版）,1998(02):89—97+130.

[53] 傅晶 , 王敏 , 梁中荟 , 等 . 泉州：宋元中国的世界海洋商贸中心——系列遗产整体价值及要素构成研究 [J]. 自然与文化遗产研究 ,2021,6(3):5—21.

图书在版编目（CIP）数据

世遗之城：宋元中国的世界海洋商贸中心：汉英对照 / 中共泉州市委宣传部编．--福州：福建人民出版社，2024.6（2025.3重印）
（世遗之城：泉州）
ISBN 978-7-211-09041-9

Ⅰ.①世… Ⅱ.①中… Ⅲ.①海上运输—丝绸之路—泉州—宋元时期—汉、英 Ⅳ.①K295.73

中国国家版本馆 CIP 数据核字（2023）第 079014 号

世遗之城——宋元中国的世界海洋商贸中心
SHIYI ZHI CHENG——SONGYUAN ZHONGGUO DE SHIJIE HAIYANG SHANGMAO ZHONGXIN

特约撰稿：丁毓玲　段燕飞
翻　　译：［加］Mei Lan Wang　洪　梅
责任编辑：李雯婷
美术编辑：陈培亮
责任校对：李雪莹
装帧设计：雅昌（上海）设计中心
出版发行：福建人民出版社　　电　　话：0591-87533169(发行部)
网　　址：http://www.fjpph.com　　电子邮箱：fjpph7211@126.com
地　　址：福州市东水路 76 号　　邮政编码：350001
经　　销：福建新华发行（集团）有限责任公司
印　　刷：雅昌文化（集团）有限公司
地　　址：深圳市南山区深云路 19 号
电　　话：0755-86083235
开　　本：787 毫米×1092 毫米　1/16
印　　张：12
字　　数：302 千字
版　　次：2024 年 6 月第 1 版
印　　次：2025 年 3 月第 2 次印刷
书　　号：ISBN 978-7-211-09041-9
定　　价：58.00 元